The Splendid Soft Toy Book

The Splendid Soft Toy Book

Search Press, London
Sterling Publishing Co., Inc., New York

First published in Great Britain 1981 by Search Press Limited, 2/10 Jerdan Place, London SW6 5PT

First published in the United States of America in 1981 by Sterling Publishing Co., Inc., 2 Park Avenue, New York, N.Y. 10016

Reprinted 1981

The original material in *The Splendid Soft Toy Book* was published in the following six volumes – text and pattern diagrams by Erna Rath, photographs by Toni Schneiders – which appeared in the Brunnen-Reihe series published by Christophorus-Verlag Herder GmbH, Freiburg im Breisgau, Federal Republic of Germany: *Stoffpuppen, Clowns und Kasperle; Neue Stoffpuppen; Puppen für Erwachsene; Stofftiere; Neue Stofftiere;* and *Tiere und Puppen aus Wolle* (also published by Search Press Limited in the Leisurecrafts Series as *Woolly Toys*).

© Christophorus-Verlag Herder GmbH 1973, 1978, 1981, 1973, 1977, 1976

Woolly Toys © Search Press Limited 1978

The Splendid Soft Toy Book © Search Press Limited 1981

ISBN 0 85532 456 2 in Great Britain

ISBN 0-8069-5448-5 in USA

Printed in USA by Connecticut Printers Inc., Bloomfield, Connecticut

INTRODUCTION

There are over 200 enchanting dolls and animals in *The Splendid Soft Toy Book* – all specially designed to appeal to children of all ages! You will find endearing baby dolls, fierce shaggy trolls, squashy soft-knitted animals to cuddle and squeeze in bed, as well as some stunning collectors' dolls which would grace the most elegant home. These are dolls which grown-ups like to own, with their beautifully made period wardrobes that recall the nostalgic memories of bygone days. At the other end of the scale are the popular 'cushion' toys, either designed with human faces or animal shapes. These are meant to be given plenty of boisterous treatment, in and out of the bedroom; and are ideal for making up in washable fabrics such as towelling or cotton prints.

The Splendid Soft Toy Book will appeal both to beginners and those who already have some experience of toymaking. For most of the designs, all you need is a working knowledge of basic sewing techniques. There are two main sections, one for dolls, the other for animals. Both start off with the simple toys first, then progress to more complex creations. In the introductory section, the basic techniques are explained in clear text and diagrams, and provide the standard patterns for most of the designs contained in the book. These are clearly identified for easy cross-reference throughout. Extra techniques such as clay modelling instructions for period dolls are given separately, as are techniques for knitting and crochet.

Once you are familiar with these standard guidelines for dolls, animals and clothing, you will find it very easy to ring the changes and invent your own variations. Indeed, these are not rigid designs which *have* to be followed, but the foundation skills of toymaking. Few crafts are so satisfying to learn, since you know that these soft toys will provide hours of pleasure and delight for their lucky owners – whether they be six or sixty!

CONTENTS

Designing

1. Dolls

Most of the dolls shown in this book are the soft, cuddly type which children love. They take no particular artistic skill to make, and require the most simple techniques of sewing, knitting or crochet. For those experienced in toymaking, some more advanced projects are included; however even these are not beyond the scope of beginners, given patience and enthusiasm. Among these are the beautiful 'decorative' dolls, dressed in silk and velvet garments which recall bygone days. These can be an attractive feature in a living room, or as part of a doll collection. Also included are jolly characters from fairy tales, and lots of different types of clown.

2. Animals

The animals are not intended to be completely realistic or faithful to nature; this would make the work extremely difficult. Some are designed to imitate natural shapes, while others are stylized, or even 'humanized'. Children identify with their soft toy companions, and readily accept them, whatever their shape or personality. Teenagers and young-at-heart adults are also fond of animal caricatures.

When designing your own animals bear in mind the following: always simplify the outline considerably; do not attempt too-accurate modelling, e.g. arms and legs. The important things to get right are the basic shape, and one or two characteristic features such as the ears or mane. For small children the shapes of the animals can be made more stylized by making the heads bigger and noses blunter; this gives very large animals a particularly dramatic, 'large as life' look.

Making up

Before starting work always read the general instructions on making up on these pages. You will find further details in the individual instructions for the dolls and animals, covering points not included in the general instructions or apparent from the illustration.

All the figures have been designed expressly to make them as simple as possible. A basic knowledge of sewing, and some knitting and crochet for the woolly toys, is all you will need. With both dolls and animals, the easiest examples are shown first, and then become gradually more difficult. If you have no experience of toy-making you should start with these simple figures. By doing so you will develop the ability to cope with the more complicated ones.

Full instructions for making four-footed animals are given on page 77, and for clothing on pages 16–18. The general instructions for animals and dolls made in wool are on pages 109–111.

Sizes

The sizes given for the finished toys are those produced when the diagram-pattern is enlarged according to the scale given on it. By making the squares smaller or larger these can be changed. Figures should not be enlarged too much without adjusting the proportions too. N.B. small figures are given a deliberately droll look with disproportionately large heads; if such patterns are over-enlarged the heads would look grotesque!

1. Dolls

When creating dolls of your own design, or copying patterns freely, observe this basic rule. A doll looks older, the smaller the head is in relation to the body. If the proportions do not turn out pleasingly you can achieve a compromise by altering the length of the legs. Most of the purely decorative and fashion dolls have longer legs, which are more true-to-life.

2. Animals

The body size given does *not* include ears and tail. The height of four-footed animals is measured from head (without ears) to foot, and the length from the tip of the nose or mouth to the rear end, minus tail. If a four-footed animal is enlarged into one designed for sitting on, take care that the legs are thick enough to bear the extra weight.

Patterns

No special artistic skill is required for enlarging the diagram-patterns to actual size; all you need is the help of a grid of squares. Start by drawing the squares on a sheet of paper in the size given. This is easiest to do using strips of stiff paper cut to the width of the square required. Lay these on the sheet of paper next to one another, at right angles. Then pencil along the edges. Next, simply transfer the outlines of the diagram-pattern onto the squares.

Where necessary, any explanations concerning individual patterns are given in the instructions for the figure in question; for four-footed animals detailed instructions on drawing patterns are given on page 77.

Often, where a pattern piece is symmetrical, only one half is shown; this is indicated by a heavy broken line. Draw this half first, then put it on a folded sheet of paper with the broken line on the fold. Then cut out a complete pattern. Cut the pattern piece out of the squared paper so that the broken fold line is still visible along the edge. Then, if necessary, several layers of paper can be cut out together. In this way, the pattern pieces can be used more than once, and it helps to work out the fabric requirements. With very thick fabrics, such as fur and fleecy textures, this method is essential since the fabric would be too bulky to cut out double.

For knitted toys, or those made from discarded knitwear, the patterns are not on a grid. They are calculated by measurements. (See pages 109–111).

The key to pattern markings is on page 111.

Materials

1. Dolls

For heads, bodies, arms and legs, felt, cotton knit, jersey and towelling in light pink or flesh color are all suitable. White fabric can be dyed to a flesh color with commercial dye; alternatively use black tea. For the clothing you can utilize all sorts of scraps left over from dressmaking, as well as garments discarded by anyone from babies to grandmothers, including knitted cotton sweatshirts, tee-shirts, knitwear, underwear, baby linen, socks, stockings and gloves. Short lengths of fabric sold cheaply in remnant sales are also useful. Felt has the advantage over fabric of being non-fraying at the edges.

2. Animals

As for dolls, use fabric scraps or discarded clothing, as well as felt. Fleecy coats can be created with the sort of fabric used for winter coat lining. A good department store will have a selection. When animals are to have a furry coat washable synthetic fur fabric is especially good, and scraps of this fabric are often available cheaply. Towelling is also suitable, especially for small children's toys. Buy this by the length, or use discarded towels. As regards choice of color there are no hard and fast rules; but most children like bright shades.

Other materials

You may be using variously sized balls made of wood, polystyrene, cellulose or plastic; scraps of leather, raffia; glue, paint and varnish, paint brushes, modelling clay. All these can be bought in craft shops, and some also in do-it-yourself shops, art shops and department stores. For braid, lace and all sewing accessories go to a good department store.

Materials used for wool figures are described on page 109. For filling materials see under Stuffing.

Materials used for hair are described under Hair Styles.

Fabric requirements

The fabric requirements given are for making the figure in the size shown. The width given allows for pattern matching and pile direction where necessary. If a 100cm (40″) width is specified, and your fabric comes in a 150cm (60″) width, for example, the remnant can be used to make another little animal, or perhaps an ear or tail.

If a doll is made out of scrap material, or by cutting up cast-off clothing, no fabric requirement is given. Simply lay the paper patterns on the fabric available or, if fabric is to be bought, on a sheet of paper. Calculate the amount required, bearing in mind broken lines indicating half-patterns, seam and hem allowances. Dolls with sewn-on clothing can have the parts of their bodies which are not visible made from any scraps available. Only heads and hands or arms need be made in flesh-colored fabric.

Cutting out

Cut out the patterns on a sheet of paper and lay them on the wrong side of the fabric. When cutting out *add an allowance of 6–10mm (¼″–⅜″) for all seams.*

With felt, plastic coated fabric and leather, which are sewn from the right side, allow only 2–3mm (¹/₁₆–⅛″). Where parts are inserted into others allow 2mm (¹/₁₆″) on these edges. The total of pieces required is always given on the key to the pattern (e.g. Body 2, Legs 4).

With fur and fur fabric attention must be paid to the direction of the pile. The pattern pieces must be laid out so that this corresponds to the natural 'lie' of the fur on a real animal. On all figures designed to be made in fur fabric, arrows on the pattern indicate the direction of the pile. Fur fabric should be cut out in a *single* layer only. It is a good idea to make as many pattern pieces as the number indicated in the key. To do this put as many sheets of pattern paper as pieces needed under the enlarged pattern and cut all the pieces out at once.

When cutting fur fabric cut only the fabric base, and with real fur cut only through the leather. Use a razor blade in a safety holder so that none of the pile is trapped.

Thin fabrics can be cut doubled over. Half-patterns, indicated by a heavy broken line, can also be cut from thin fabric in this way: fold the fabric with the grain lines running parallel and place the broken line edge of the pattern against the fold.

The drawing *(a)* shows how to cut out matching pieces by folding fabric right sides together. Place the pattern pieces in position, then cut out. Remember to include the seam allowances. Another method *(b)* is to cut out two pattern pieces, and lay them on a single piece of the fabric, again allowing for seams. In the case of close-piled fabrics, which do not have a grain, animal head panels can be cut out all in one piece. However, if the fabric used is furry, and has a natural grain, the panels must be cut in two sections *(c)*. The hairs at the top of the head and the back of the neck must lie backwards, and those on the front of the head forwards, following the arrows in the pattern.

See also under Patterns, page 9, and Cutting out clothing pieces, page 16.

Sewing

Lay the pieces right sides together and sew on the wrong side, by machine or by hand, with small running stitches or back stitches.

Identical pieces are always joined together, e.g. body, head, ears, arms, hands, feet, unless there are one or more inset panels to go between them. This occurs on the heads of many dolls and animals, and the bodies of animals.

If darts are indicated close these first. Set soles for dolls' and animals' feet into openings left for them after sewing up the legs.

With all pieces openings must be left for turning and stuffing, wherever possible in the least conspicuous places, or ones which will be covered by another part, e.g. a head, body, arm, leg, tail or ear.

Animals with a body inset panel can also be left open at the belly.

After sewing, clip into the seam allowance at corners and curves, stopping just short of the stitching *(d)*, and then trim the seam to about 6mm (¼″) wide or 2mm (¹/₁₆″) for very small pieces.

Sew leather and felt pieces on the right side, the seams running close to the edges, using either running stitches *(e)* or small overcasting stitches *(f)*.

After turning the pieces out stuff and sew the various parts together by hand with invisible stitches; close any remaining openings.

For sewing clothes see pages 16–17.

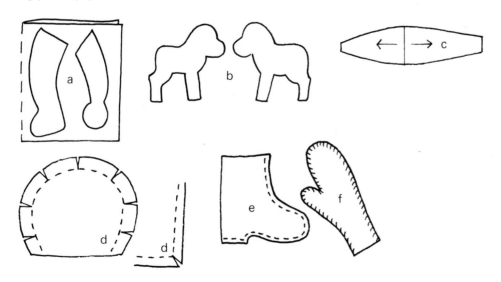

Arm and leg rolls

A way to save on stuffing is to make arm and leg rolls from the fleecy fabric used to line coats in winter, or a thick pile type fabric (a). Check the fabrics that are available in department stores. These rolls will be covered over in fabric, or the doll's clothes can be sewn on over them. Tight rolls are only needed if the doll has to stand; usually they can be quite loose in texture. To shape the limbs, sew darts or pleats at the knee and elbow joints by hand, (b). The limbs can be tucked into prepared hands, feet, shoes or gloves, whichever is used.

Stuffing

Suitable materials

Filling material can be obtained in department stores, craft shops and from upholsterers. Synthetic fibre fillings and foam chips wash well, even in the washing machine, so long as the rest of the toy will stand up to this. Foam chips should not be too coarse or they will look unsightly through thin fabric. It is possible to cut them into smaller pieces. Kapok, cotton waste or the insides of old pillows or cushions should only be used for dolls and animals which are not intended to be washed. You can also use cut-up tights or soft fabric scraps as stuffing, and with very large animals, even woodshavings. A way of both minimizing stuffing and using up fabric remnants is shown in the drawing and caption (left).

How to stuff

Proper stuffing is vital to the look and shape of any cuddly toy. Even the most carefully made doll will look pathetic if it is carelessly stuffed. With loose and uneven stuffing the legs will sag together, and creases appear in the head. Only dolls and animals intended as cushions and pillows, or as bed-time toys, should be lightly stuffed.

With large animals specially designed for sitting on neither stuffing nor effort should be spared. You may need to enlist the help of the man of the family here.

Put stuffing in layer by layer; work very carefully, making sure right from the start that there are no gaps or lumps, as these cannot be corrected afterwards.

The greatest care is needed with dolls' heads, which must be very tightly and smoothly stuffed.

A kitchen spoon, knitting needle or the point of a pair of scissors will help to penetrate into the tip of small parts, but take care not to pierce the material!

Heads

1. Dolls' Heads

Fabric heads are usually made with two identical pieces cut from a pattern, with or without darts or a centre panel. With very simple dolls they are cut all in one with the body.

If the bodies have long necks, these are sewn firmly to the back of the head (A).

Flexible dolls with wired-rope skeletons (pages 58–63) can have heads made from wood, cellulose, polystyrene or plastic balls. These are sometimes shaped by adding cotton wool wound around with thread (B). Similar ball heads can also be used on some dolls and animals made from wool.

Heads made from a variety of materials can be covered with knitted cotton, jersey or felt. This is done by cutting out a round piece, large enough to envelop the whole head.

A row of running stitches around the edge (C) allows it to be very tightly drawn together after being put over the head. The folds that appear are pushed to the back, and the surplus sewn up vertically (back view D).

This covering is put on before fastening together the head and neck (except on wired-rope figures). The neck too has a covering of the same fabric, either made from a straight strip, or cut from a pattern, and a little stuffing is inserted under it.

The modelling of heads from self-hardening clay is explained in detail on pages 52–54, with pictures.

2. Animals' Heads

These can either be in one with the body, or made up separately and sewn on, in the same way as for dolls. Sometimes the heads are in profile.

Dolls' Faces

To make sure the finished face is symmetrical, divide the head into sections with tacking or basting stitches before sewing the pieces together (E).

If a face is drawn on the pattern this can be transferred to the fabric with tacking or basting stitches, stitching through the outlines and lines on the pattern piece.

As the final shape may be altered by the stuffing, try out the position of the features with bits of paper, felt and yarn. With dolls try on the hair as well. Then you can finally put them in position.

Features can be embroidered (F), or made from felt, leather, buttons and balls, glued or sewn on (G).

On toys for small children no balls or buttons should be used because they might tear them off and swallow them.

If the toy is to be washable it is important to test the color-fastness of all features beforehand.

If a lot of toys are being made a punch is useful, so that round features can be made quickly. Punches can be bought at craft shops and some department stores.

On smooth fabrics it is possible to paint directly on the face with fabric or acrylic paint; acrylic and poster colors can also be used on clay-modelled and wooden heads (see page 54).

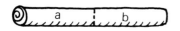

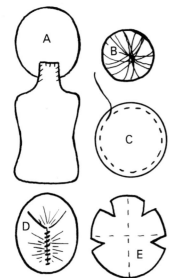

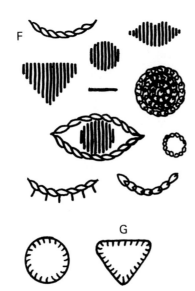

The features are either given on the pattern, or measurements and diameters are given in the text.

For eyes, the larger piece or number is for the eye, the smaller piece is for the pupil.

Dolls' Eyes

Contrary to the proportions of a real human face these are larger than the mouth. Often a simple disk is sufficient (a). An arch can be embroidered over this (b). When the eyes consist of two disks, the smaller ones must both be placed in the same position (c). Eyes in style d have a round iris in the centre, the larger ones also have a pupil (e). Clowns' eyes can be a different shape (f/g). A white highlight gives a lively look to all eyes. This should be placed in the same spot for both eyes, either by embroidering two stitches close together, or painting a dot (h).

Closed or sleeping eyes are shown by a curved line (i).

Dolls' Noses

On small dolls it is sufficient to indicate these with pink dots, lines or disks (j, k).

On fabric heads little balls or fabric-covered buttons (made as for animals' eyes, t) can be sewn on.

Noses lying under the 'skin' are pushed in through a cut made in the upper forehead.

To do this smear the ball with glue, insert the point of a pair of scissors into the hole and push it into the right position between the stuffing and fabric.

The ball should be suspended from a few threads (l). A cone-shaped nose is made in the same way, using a matchstick wrapped around with cotton wool bound on with thread (m).

Until the glue dries the position of the nose can be changed by manipulating the threads.

Dolls' Mouths

These can be embroidered or glued on, either straight or curved (n); they can be round (o); or in shape p with or without satin stitching on top (when doing this take the thread right through to the back of the head).

Shape q is for a negro face; r for a clown: it indicates make-up, and is white with a red mouth line in the centre.

Cheeks

These can be embroidered in various ways, sewn on, shaded on with colored pencil or rouge, or painted.

Animals' Faces

Animals' Eyes

These can be the same as many of the dolls' eyes or the animals' eyes s with pupils on the upper or lower edge.

Ball buttons or fabric-covered buttons can also be used.

To cover a button cut out a disk of fabric about twice as large as the eye size required, then draw it up tightly with a gathering thread (t), put in the button and secure with criss-cross stitching on the back.

If the eyes are white put small black disks on top. Large animals can have eyes consisting of several disks (u).

Animals' Noses and Mouths

The pictures v show different types of nose; simple noses can also be made by embroidering a V shape.

Embroidered mouths (w), or ones made with 'shoe-lace' cord, can have an outline shape added to them, made of one or two arcs (x). On deep-pile fabrics use thick yarn or wool.

In addition pompons and buttons can be used; these can be covered as required (see t under Animals' Eyes above).

Noses can also be made with round pieces of fabric gathered up and stuffed. Several animals have nostrils (y) or a nose sewn from one or two pattern pieces.

Animals' Ears

These strongly influence the appearance of the face, so they too should be tried out until they look just right. The insides can be made in contrasting fabric. Gather them slightly where they join the head, or make small pleats.

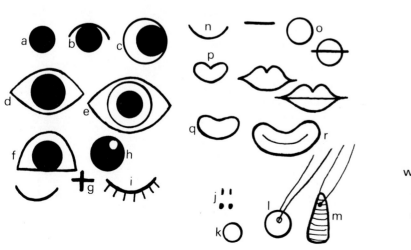

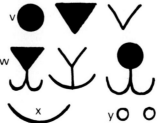

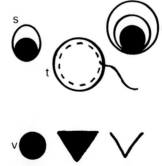

Hair for dolls and animals

Wool hair

The small letters refer to the individual styles. The Roman figures I-IV refer to the pictures showing how the different styles are placed on the head.

a/b Fringe: sew lengths of wool onto a tape and secure to the head *(al)*; or bind together in the middle and sew on in the same place.

b Bundle of wool as a beard: sew lengths of wool bound together in the centre underneath the nose.

c Short hair style: (short to shoulder length): sew the wool to a tape as shown, so that the shorter ends cover the forehead, the longer ones cover the head. Part *d* goes on over this.

d Long and short hair style: sew strands to the required length to a tape in the centre and secure to the head, possibly covering with a fringe. (See picture II showing both long and short style).

e Full short hair style (short to shoulder length): make up two parts as under *a*, and sew to the sides of the head (I). Cover with part *d*.

f Simple short or long hair style, also clown's hair: bind the lengths of wool together in the centre, sew the bundle to the centre of the head and distribute the strands.

If you wish, shorten some strands to make a fringe (see also drawing *f*). For a clown place one bundle on each side of the head.

g, h, i Mop head: sew on small bundles of wool, made with straight lengths *(g)* or loops *(h)*, in close rows (III).

Alternatively draw lengths of wool through the head fabric with a crochet hook to make a loop, draw the ends through the loop and tighten *(i)*. Make close rows in this way.

j Curly head: using single or double strands of wool take a back stitch in the head, leaving a loop, then make another backstitch without a loop. Continue in this way.

k Circle of hair or beard: for bald heads, or ones with sewn-on hats, or for beards, mark out a line with basting or tacking stitches and sew doubled lengths of wool along it (IV and *k*).

l Crinkly hair: dampen the wool and arrange it into several thin braids, allow to dry well and undo the braids. Alternatively use wool unpicked from a garment.

m Twisted braids: sew the wool to a tape as in *d*, divide into strands, bind together, twist, stick the ends into the braid and secure.

n (no picture): the hairstyles shown in *f* and *k* on this page and *i* on page 15 are also possible using teased-out wool (only on small decorative dolls).

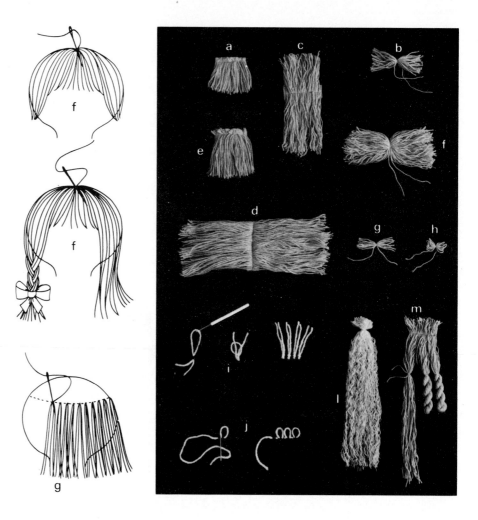

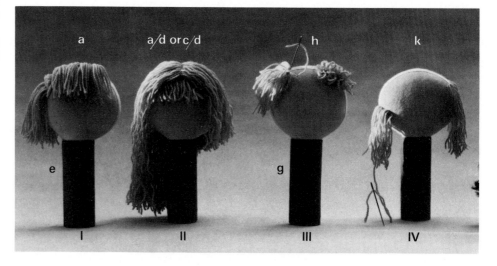

Dolls' hair

Many different materials can be used to make hair for the dolls in this book. They are wearing wigs made from wool, artificial hair, hemp – some even have wigs made from fur fabric. You can also buy lovely wigs from shops selling toymaking accessories. Splendid wigs can be made by recycling cast-off ladies' hair-pieces – see if a friend has one, or look in jumble sales etc.

Dyeing the hair
Wool, hemp and artificial hair can also be dyed – very strong black tea is often effective. However, not all materials will take the dye, so don't be disappointed. Before immersing your 'wig' material, tie it into a very loose skein to make sure the dye penetrates properly. Lengths for hair-styles are not given, as this depends on what material you have to use. If a hair-style is complicated, then more detail is given.

Shaping
Cut and shape the hair after glueing or sewing to the head. If a hat is sewn on, you only need hair where it shows. If you are cutting wigs, make sure you buy ones with a stretchy net base or border. By cutting into the edges of the base (not the hair itself) and making darts, you can reduce the size of the wig to fit your doll.

Hair-styles in artificial hair, hemp and fur

a Glue a long piece of artificial hair onto a tape about 1.5cm (⅝″) wide, reaching from the forehead to the centre of the back of the head. When the glue has dried make a parting with two rows of stitching, close together.

b To make a fringe put some hair onto a short tape as in a, and fix to the head before adding part a.

c/d To curl artificial hair dampen it and put it on hair rollers.

d To make it crinkly put it into small tight braids. But not all types of artificial hair respond in this way.

e Before using hemp for styles a, b, e, f or g, brush it out well. To make curls wind small sections (dry) around a knitting needle several times.

f For short hair bind the bundle around the centre, spread out the strands, perhaps shortening at the front for a fringe.

g Make a bundle as for f, then make a crown with a circle of fabric gathered up around the edge and glue on; shorten at front if required.

h If the hair is not long enough for method a, glue and sew it onto tapes *(h1)* then sew the tapes together *(h2)*.

i/j For dolls with attached head coverings or bald heads fasten on short lengths secured to a tape, as in a, or a strip of fur or fur fabric, around the back of the head.

k Cut a strip out of a curly wig and make up as in i, or gather up one long edge and sew on (do not catch the hair into the seam).

l Cut the crown out of a lady's wig and gather the edges with running stitches (1). Cut the hair very carefully from the wrong side only. In addition another strip can be cut off (2) and sewn to Part 1. The length of the strip should be about ¾ × the circumference of part 1.

m (no picture) Where patterns are given, wigs can be made from fur fabric or fur scraps (for cutting see page 11). Care must be taken to see that the direction of the pile runs downwards; or use curly-pile fabric.

Animals' hair, manes, tails and braids

For single tufts of hair sew on a bundle of wool on raffia, bound around the middle (see picture f page 14). Tails and tail tassels are also made in this way.

When an animal has bushy hair or a luxuriant mane, sew on several of these bundles close together in rows.

If the animal is made of loosely woven fabric, or is knitted, hair and manes can be knotted on with wool or raffia (see i page 14); or the whole animal can be given a shaggy pelt by doing this all over.

Raffia can be moulded into the desired shape by damping it. Wool can also be unwound and teased out so that it looks like a fuzzy coat. The length of hair made in i or f can be given a final trimming.

Tufts of hair, tail tassels and manes can also be made from fur fabric or fur; to cut see page 11.

For braided parts like tails, feelers and little legs draw lengths of wool, yarn or raffia (any number divisible by three) through the fabric with a darning needle, braid, finish with a knot and unwind braid at the bottom to form a tassel.

Clothing

Instructions for making nearly all items of clothing needed in the book are given here. Anything not included or which is different from the standard method, will be found in the instructions given with the photograph of the particular doll or animal.

Cutting out

Place patterns with a heavy broken line on doubled fabric, folded with the grain straight, so that the line is on the fold (1).

When cutting out *add seam allowances of 6–10mm (1/4"–3/8"); 10mm (3/8") for shoulder seams.*

In addition allow 2cm (3/4") for an elasticated hem, for hems on frills 1.5cm (5/8"), on the lower edges of skirts, smocks, dresses and coats 3cm (11/8"), on sleeves and trouser legs 2cm (3/4").

Where lace or frills are to be added, omit the hem allowance; likewise for felt clothing, and edges in knitting or leather.

Where measurements are given instead of a pattern (e.g. for skirts, frills, straps, pinafores, waist and neck bands) the above allowances are already included.

Two identical pieces are always used, except where dresses, bodices, blouses, smocks and pullovers have overlapping edges to allow for button fastening.

In this case, depending on whether this is at front or back, one pattern piece is cut twice and the other once.

If the pattern has a heavy broken line at the shoulders, the garment consists of a single piece with a neck opening cut in the middle.

If two neck openings are shown the deeper one is the front.

Facings and Hems

Facings for button fastening should be turned under along the line on the pattern.

Hems can be made by hand or machine. First turn the edge very narrowly under, then turn again to the hem width.

Gathering

Gathering can be done either by hand with running stitches, or using the longest stitch on the sewing machine (pull the bobbin thread on machine gathering).

If the fabric is only very lightly gathered, in order to ease it onto another piece, gathering is not essential, but always makes things easier.

If the gathering is to be very tight, as on a ruff, use two rows of gathering threads, about 5mm (1/4") apart; draw them both up together and even the gathers out as required.

For narrow lace, sleeves and trouser legs, one row is sufficient.

On skirts, pinafores and frills the opposite edge should be hemmed first. For frills allow 1½ to 3 times the length of the edge on which the frill is to be set.

Closure and Neck Fastenings

Smocks, shirts, blouses, pullovers and dresses which consist of two identical parts need a vertical slit down centre back (2). This is finished with a bias strip, or has a facing piece to turn under, or is narrowly hemmed.

Usually a button and loop fastening is sufficient, or ties. You can also stitch lace or a band onto the neck edge and thread a cord through to draw it up.

With wide dresses, and smocks with sufficiently large neck openings, no slit is necessary.

Baby doll jackets are cut right down the back, narrowly hemmed and given a tie fastening.

On edges with facings, and bodices made from double fabric, make the closing with buttons and buttonholes or loops; alternatively, use press-studs.

Skirts and pinafores are fastened on the waistband, or are tied together at the back with extended waistband strips.

Find the position required for the fastening by trying the garment on.

To make neck bands, cut a bias strip (one set at right angles to the grain of the fabric unless it is jersey) twice the width required plus seam allowance.

Sew it to the neck, right sides together, then turn the free edge to the inside and sew down (3).

Wide neck openings can be gathered up before setting on a band or lace (4).

Lace (gathered or plain) can either be sewn directly onto the neck edge, or to a neck band.

On small items of clothing it is sufficient to hem the edge neck with running stitches, leaving the ends long enough to tie.

Collars and Clowns' Ruffs

Collars made of felt consist of one layer; those made of fabric need two layers, sewn together and turned out. Lace collars can be lightly or tightly gathered.

Ruffs can be made with lace, voile, tulle or ribbon and lace and should be as tightly gathered as possible. You can also put one ruff on top of another.

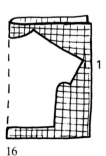

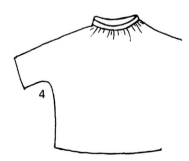

'Kimono' Patterns

This is the name for a very simple pattern in which the sleeves are made in one with the body.

The front and back pieces are joined with seams at the shoulders (unless a heavy broken line indicates a fold) and sides which continue to form the sleeves.

Both long and short kimono sleeves are gathered 1.5–3cm (⅝"–1⅛") away from the ends; or sew in elastic.

Clothes with Set-in Sleeves

Sew front and back pieces together at the shoulders and then set in the sleeves (centre meeting the shoulder seam).

Wide sleeves should be gathered at the top first so that they fit into the armhole.

Finally close sleeve and side seams as one (5). These sleeves can be gathered too (see under Kimono Patterns).

Skirts, Pinafore Skirts, Pinafore Dresses and Petticoats

The lengths and widths given should only be taken as a guide, and should be altered according to your taste and the fabric available.

Close the skirt strip into a circle, leaving a slit for pulling on (6—seam = centre back).

With pinafore skirts, instead of sewing the edges together just hem them.

Gather up the waist edge, then, for skirts and aprons, set on a doubled waistband.

For dresses, pinafores and pinafore dresses sew to the bodice or yoke.

For straps, sew turned-out fabric 'tubes' to the skirt or pinafore waistband.

An underskirt is made just like a skirt, but with an elasticated waist and no openings.

Only decide final skirt lengths after trying the garment on the doll; hem the edge or trim with a frill or lace.

Pinafores and Pinafore Dresses

For the yoke cut one piece in main fabric, and one in lining fabric; otherwise use two pieces of the main fabric.

Join the two layers at the shoulders, then sew neck and back edges, right sides together, turn out, turn the armhole edges under narrowly and sew together.

For skirt pieces see under Skirts.

Trousers and Pants

On trousers with a heavy broken line on the pattern close the front and back centre seams (7), lay the two pieces together and sew the inner leg seams (8).

On trousers made in four pieces also sew the sides (9). Insert elastic in the waist.

Simple trousers: lay the two pieces together and close the inside leg seam (10) and the outside seams (11) after clipping. Underpants can be made in this way without a pattern.

Otherwise, use a trouser pattern, adjusting the leg length and width as required. Trim the bottoms with lace.

Wide legs should be gathered up (12).

Romper Suits, Tights, Simple Trousers from Knitwear

Romper suits or tights can be made with discarded socks or cut-off sleeves from sweaters.

Cut both layers out of the knitted 'tube' and sew together as in 10 so as to make two legs, finishing the sole edges.

Short woollen trousers can be made in the same way; otherwise knit a tube and sew it together with a few stitches at the crotch (13).

Provide all woollen trousers with elastic at the waist.

Stockings and Socks

To make long stockings either lengthen the pattern above, or just sew up simple tubes.

Stretch the bottom edges when sewing together (14).

If shoes are to be sewn in place just draw the tube together at the bottom after putting on (see also below).

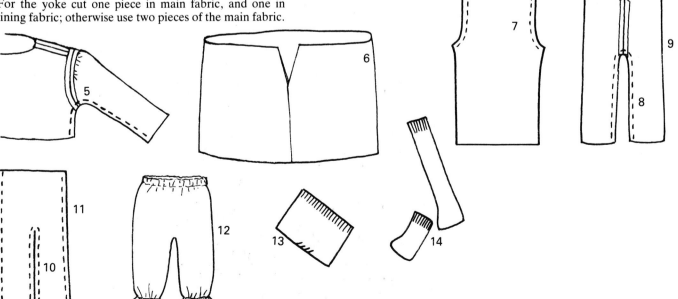

Using Discarded Knitwear

When cutting out pullovers, dresses, caps, tights and socks from discarded knitwear, place the patterns against the edges of the garment so as to take advantage of the ribbing.

If it is too wide it can be turned under.

Sew the seams by hand or machine with very small stitches to make sure of catching in all the knitted stitches.

Set bands of ribbing onto the neck edges to make stand-up collars or polo necks.

Shoes

As well as scraps of felt and leather, discarded leather goods such as bags, gloves and wallets can be turned into shoes.

If sewing by hand on the right side allow a 2mm ($^1/_{12}$") seam allowance.

If sewing right sides together allow 4mm ($^1/_6$").

First sew the upper parts together, on boots only as far as the mark shown.

Unless stated otherwise, the soles should be set in with the wider end at the front.

Shoes without soles are sewn together underneath. On lace-up shoes pierce or punch holes with a hole punch and thread with thonging, ribbon, yarn or wool.

Sewn-on shoes can have an embroidered purely decorative fastening (15) baby bootees a woollen drawstring (16).

Sewn-on Clothing

Clothes can be sewn onto all dolls intended to be purely decorative, or if they are designed to be washed clothes and all.

To do this make a vertical cut in the upper part of the back, and after drawing the garment over the body turn the cut edges under narrowly and sew them together.

If the neck has a wide opening gather it up after putting the head through.

Gather skirts, petticoats, trousers and pants and sew to the body, or upper part of the clothing.

Cover the join either with overgarments, a velvet ribbon or a band of doubled fabric.

Other garments, shoes, hats and bonnets can also be sewn in place, provided the stitches are invisible.

Hats and Bonnets

Bonnets with ruched edges

Either cut two pattern pieces (sometimes in different fabrics), sew and turn out along the front, curved edge; alternatively, cut one piece and trim this edge with lace. Then sew the darts, hem the lower edge or sew the two layers together, gather up to fit and add ties.

Caps and Clown's Hats

If the cap consists of one piece sew together down centre back.

If it has two pieces sew at the sides and top.

If it has four pieces sew sides, front and back seams.

Except when felt is used, neaten the edges with a bias strip, or make a hem; on peaked caps include the peak.

Crochet Hat

The hat takes two skeins of 'craft raffia' for a large doll, using a No. 4 (F) crochet hook; or for a small doll a No. 2 (I) hook. The following numbers 1) to 15) indicate the number of rows. (U.S. readers use s.c. throughout).

First close 4 chain into a circle and continue in double crochet. 1) work 10dc into the ring, 2) work 2 dc into each dc, 3) work 2 dc into every 2nd dc, 4) work 2 dc into every 3rd dc, 5) work 2 dc into every 4th dc, 6) and 7) work 2 dc into every 7th dc, 8) to 13) continue without picking up, 14) work 2 dc into every 4th dc, 15) work 2 dc into every 5th dc and continue to crochet until the desired size is reached.

The hat will turn out larger or smaller although the number of rows is the same according to whether a thick or thin hook is used.

Shaped Felt Hat

Cut the brim with the pattern. If the felt is thin, glue two layers together.

To make the crown use a circle of felt, dampen it and place it over a tubular shaped container such as a glass, and secure with a rubber band (see photograph).

The diameter of the 'mould' should be about the same as the inner curve of the brim.

When dry, cut the crown along the line of the rubber band, sew it to the brim and hide the join with a decorative band or piece of braid (17).

Four mascots

These little mascots – a dwarf, a clown and two troll children – take very little time to make, yet have masses of charm. They are about the size of the palm of your hand, and have simple, oval-shaped bodies. This is an ideal way of using up scraps of felt and oddments of wool. Since felt does not fray, it is easy to hand-sew, and even quite small children have no trouble making up the designs. This is also a good opportunity to practise ways of placing eyes, noses and mouths to create a range of different facial expressions.

Four mascots

1 = Body × 2
2 = Arm × 2
3 = Leg × 2
4 = Face × 1
5 = Eye (for clown) × 2
6 = Cheek × 2
7 = Nose × 1
8 = Mouth × 1
9 = Dwarf's cap × 1
10 = Hat piece (for clown at front) × 1
11 = Hat piece (for clown at back) × 1
.... = Wool set on here

Four Mascots

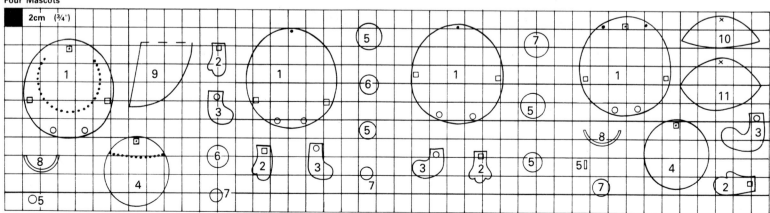

2cm (¾")

Four mascots

Cut out the pattern pieces, using the key provided.

To make up the design, follow the general instructions on pages 8–18. Be sure to check any special instructions and techniques used for this pattern. Any extra information is supplied as needed below.

Only the bodies are stuffed, the arms and legs consist of a single layer.

If you wish you can cut these out double, sew them together and stuff.

Cut the bodies out of pieces of felt without adding any seam allowance and sew the wrong sides together, close along the edge, using embroidery thread. This makes the stitches decorative in themselves.

Place the arms and legs in between the body pieces so that they are secured by the body seam.

The dwarf and clown have round white faces; for the dwarf attach short lengths of wool underneath for the beard, then glue on hair and cap.

The two storybook trolls, boy and girl, have woolly wigs, and the clown has bundles of wool fastened to the sides of his head (see *f*, page 14). Finally glue on the jolly features.

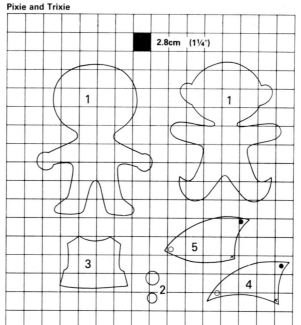

Pixie and Trixie

2.8cm (1¼")

Pixie and Trixie

1 = Body and Head × 2
2 = Eye × 2
3 = Dress × 2
4 = Front cap × 1
5 = Back cap × 1

Pixie and Trixie

This cheeky pair of characters are cut out all in one piece from felt. Again, children who have basic sewing skills will find them easy to make, using running stitches for the outline seams. Pixie and Trixie are about 20cm (8") high, and what's more they can be dressed like 'proper' dolls – a simple smock and smart pixie hat are provided in the pattern.

Bill and Ben

These delightful black and white baby dolls are 29cm (11½") high, and dressed in simple shirt and dungarees. In the picture, Bill and Ben are made up in felt, but if you want to wash the dolls, they look good in towelling too. Remember to choose washable stuffing material! For the first time, you are shown how to cut the head separately from the body – a method used for many other dolls in this book. Also there are hints on adapting the basic clothes patterns to make other items in the babies' wardrobes.

Remember that when you are making your own soft toys at home, you are not in competition with the mass-produced doll that walks, talks and sings! Yours may not be a glittering example of high technology, but children soon get bored with these toys anyway. The dolls and animals in this book are mostly uncomplicated and supremely cuddly playthings, which are meant to be hugged and squeezed with great gusts of affection. Children who do not settle to sleep easily are often helped to feel more secure if they can sleep with a favourite toy. Boys should never be discouraged from having a doll on the grounds that it is 'sissy' to own one. Left to their own devices, they will leave their cars and trains standing, and take a whole family of soft creatures into their care.

Pixie and Trixie (picture page 21)

Cut out the pattern pieces, using the key provided.

To make up the design, follow the general instructions on pages 8–18. Be sure to check any special instructions and techniques used for this pattern. Any extra information is supplied as needed below.

In this simple pattern the head and body are all one piece. If the pixie is to have a flesh-colored head he can easily be put together from separate head and body pieces.

As with the felt figures on page 20 these dolls are cut without seam allowance and sewn around the edge, wrong sides together, with a running stitch.

If the mouths are to be embroidered by children mark them out with strong thread.

Make the woolly wigs as style *f*, page 14.

The doll has an equally easy-to-sew smock with a drawstring at the neck; the pixie just has a broderie anglaise lace ruff and a pointed cap and is decorated with two buttons.

A smock sewn from the doll's pattern would also suit him.

Bill and Ben Baby dolls

Cut out the pattern pieces, using the key provided.

To make up the design, follow the general instructions on pages 8–18. Be sure to check any special instructions and techniques used for this pattern. Any extra information is supplied as needed below.

The head is cut out separately and set onto the neck, so that the chin sticks forward, thus giving the head a shaped appearance although it is actually flat. This way of setting on the head is used on many other dolls in this book.

As there is so little hair it is worth going to the trouble of knotting it on (white baby) or sewing on loops of wool (black baby). See *i* and *j* on page 14.

Each needs only three rows of fringe or loops, set close together.

When sewing felt shirts and dungarees like the ones shown here there is no need to neaten the edges.

If using fabric add on a seam allowance when you cut out. See page 11.

The simple kimono-style pattern used for the shirt (open at the back) can also be used to make a dress, jacket and overcoat (open at the front), so that the baby quickly acquires a complete wardrobe.

Shoes can be made with the leg pattern drawn about 4mm (1/6″) larger.

By cutting the dungaree pattern off at the waist, you can make underpants which look most charming made in the same fabric as a little dress and peeping out from underneath it.

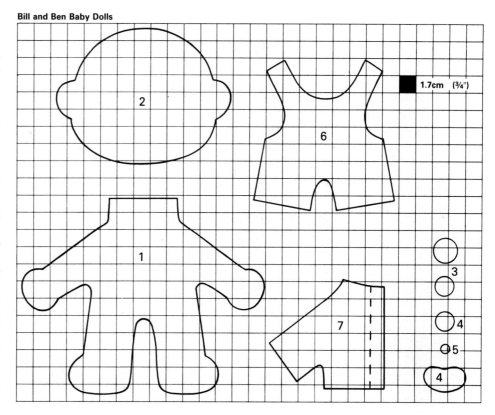

Bill and Ben Baby Dolls

1.7cm (¾″)

Bill and Ben

1 = Body × 2
2 = Head × 2
3 = Eye × 2
4 = Mouth × 1
5 = Nose × 1
6 = Trousers × 2
7 = Shirt × 2 with broken line to outer edge

23

Olaf and Olga troll dolls

These shaggy troll dolls are very popular, and can be made with or without clothes. They are 45cm (18″) high, and are often used as car cushions! Trolls are good soft toys for boys who think that dolls are 'sissy'. They are simple and quick to make, and look best in fleecy or furry fabrics. In fact this is a good opportunity to practise working with thicker materials that occur more often later in the animals' section. Don't be afraid to enhance the rough and wild characteristics of these funny creatures, since this is what children love most about their troll friends. If you don't want to buy special furry fabric, you could use up old fleecy coat linings or baby clothes.

Olaf and Olga Troll Dolls

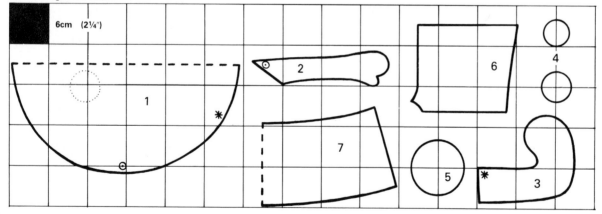

Olaf and Olga
1 = Body × 2
2 = Arm × 4
3 = Leg × 4
4 = Eye × 2
5 = Nose × 1
6 = Trousers × 4
7 = Skirt × 4

Olaf and Olga troll dolls

Cut out the pattern pieces, using the key provided.

To make up the design, follow the general instructions on pages 8–18. Be sure to check any special instructions and techniques used for this pattern. Any extra information is supplied as needed below.

Cut the pieces from fur fabric or thick fleecy material (see page 11). Sew and stuff arms and legs, and insert them in position on main body. Sew firmly. Stuff body, keeping the surface fairly flat.

The big noses are made by gathering the round pattern piece up until it measures 6cm (¼″) diameter. Then they are stuffed.

The skirt is made from double fabric.

Sew each pair of pieces together down the centre front and back, turn the two layers out along the lower seam edge and finish the waist edge with a bias band.

For the trousers, thread elastic through the back waist seam.

Make the straps from strips of fabric, or use gaily colored braid.

Hair: as under *f*, page 14 (in front only). Alternatively sew on a piece of shaggy fur.

24

Hansel and Gretel

Here are two friendly cushion dolls with invitingly wide bodies to snuggle up in. They are both 40cm (15¾") high, and can be made in a wide range of fabrics. They also have the 'ready dressed' look, and are very popular bedtime companions. Many children use these dolls as pillows to sleep upon instead of ordinary ones.

Hansel and Gretel

Cut out the pattern pieces, using the key provided overleaf.

To make up the design, follow the general instructions on pages 8–18. Be sure to check any special instructions and techniques used for this pattern. Any extra information is supplied as needed below.

First join head and body pieces and sew together the front and back.

Decorate with braid and lace, leaving openings at the arms.

Sew the hand pieces together, turn out and stuff slightly.

After stuffing the body, place the stuffed hands in the arm openings and sew securely.

These big flat faces offer plenty of possibilities for different expressions; although the head is flat the big cheeks give the faces a chubby look.

To make the woollen hair see *f* page 14; on the girl, cut a few strands short at the front to make a fringe.

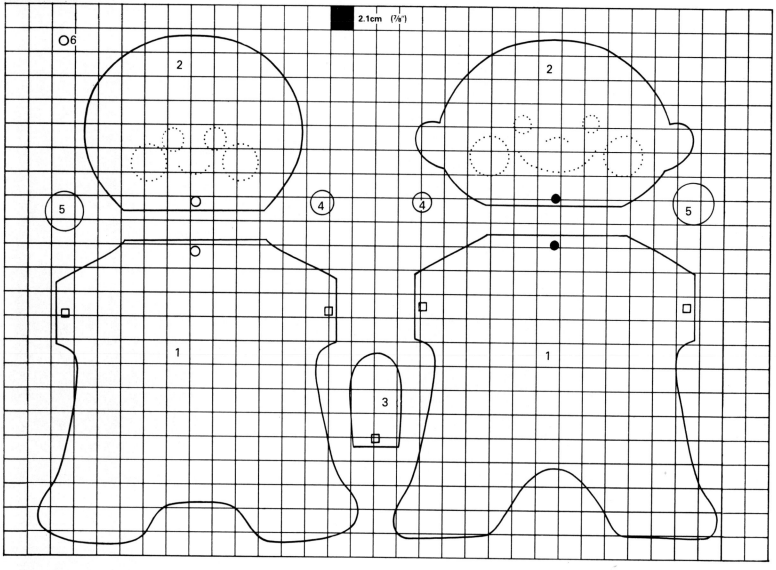

2.1cm (⁷⁄₈″)

Hansel and Gretel
1 = Body × 2
2 = Head × 2
3 = Hand × 4
4 = Eye × 2
5 = Cheek × 2
6 = Nose × 1

Sleepy pixie and doll
1 = Body × 2
2 = Head × 2
3 = Ear × 4
4 = Arm × 4
5 = Hand × 4
6 = Pixie's cap × 2
7 = Doll's mob cap × 1
8 = Pinafore × 1

Sleepy Pixie and Girl Doll

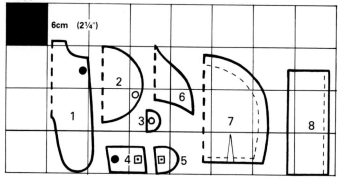

6cm (2¼″)

Sleepy Pixie and Little Girl doll

Each of these appealing 25cm (9¾") tall dolls is made up in towelling. This not only serves as the main body fabric, but also acts as the dolls' clothes – they look 'ready dressed'. For the prettiest effect choose the most delicate fabric design that you can find, since you need tiny patterns for dolls. Clever use of ribbon trim and tiny oddments of fabric to make the little pinafore means that even the smallest scraps of fabric can be used up. Sleepy dolls are excellent for encouraging children to sail off to dreamland. Notice that the pixie's cheeks are embroidered as well as the rest of his features.

Sleepy Pixie and Little Girl doll

Cut out the pattern pieces, using the key provided.

To make up the design, follow the general instructions on pages 8–18. Be sure to check any special instructions and techniques used for this pattern. Any extra information is supplied as needed below.

As the arms, hands and ears on the pixie are firmly anchored by machine stitching, making up should be done in the following sequence:

Sew the ears together, and turn inside out.

The straight edge is incorporated between the head pieces while sewing up the head of the pixie (the doll has no ears).

Place the head pieces right sides together, and slip the ears in position between them facing inwards.

Stitch up the head and ear seams all together.

Turn right side out and stuff the head.

Sew the hands together, turn and stuff lightly; place between the arm pieces so that the straight edges are incorporated while sewing up the arms.

Turn the arms out, stuff, place between the body pieces and incorporate as before while sewing up the body.

Turn the body, stuff and secure the neck to the back of the head.

Make the cap and sew to the head.

The doll is made the same way, without the ears.

For the doll cut pinafore straps and waistband, 11 × 3.5cm (4¼" × 1⅜") and 9 × 3.5cm (3½" × 1⅜") respectively, to go with the skirt pattern.

Sew the finished pinafore to the body.

Hair: Sew two rows of wool or yarn loops to the doll's head. For the pixie, knot on some fringing (see *i* and *j*, page 14).

Faces: Make the doll's eyes from 10mm (⅜") diameter circles, cheeks from 20mm (¾") diameter circles.

Embroider the same-size cheeks on the pixie, and his closed eyes.

Baby doll family

This enchanting group of three baby dolls are cut all in one piece, and the faces are sewn on separately. Like the dolls shown above, the fabric chosen for the body also looks like clothes – either a sweet little sleeping bag suit, or a baby-grow type jump suit. Choose pretty trimmings to show off the fabric. These dolls would look good made up in brushed cotton or cotton prints, as well as in towelling – in fact any fabric that is both soft to hold and easy to wash.

Baby Doll Family

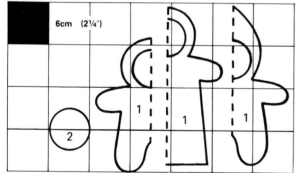

6cm (2¼″)

Baby doll family
1 = Body and Head × 2
2 = Face × 1

Baby doll family

Cut out the pattern pieces, using the key provided.

To make up the design, follow the general instructions on pages 8–18. Be sure to check any special instructions and techniques used in this pattern. Any extra information is supplied as needed below.

In all three dolls the body, head, arms and legs are cut all in one piece. The face is sewn on separately.

After sewing together the front and back pieces turn out through the face opening.

Turn under the edges of the face circle ½cm (¼″) to the inside.

Hem the edges neatly. After stuffing sew on the face and embroider it.

The eyes are 5mm (¼″) across. Finally, embroider hair with long stitches and decorate with lace and other trimmings, whatever you have available.

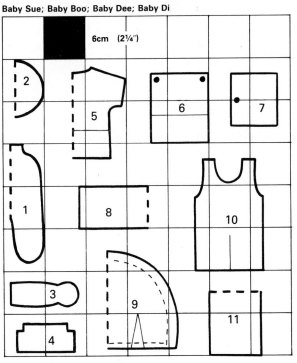

Baby Sue, Baby Boo, Baby Dee, Baby Di

This is another group of dolls which are made from the same basic pattern. They are 23cm (9″) tall, and are best made in a really soft and stretchy fabric like jersey or knitted cotton. The dolls can be made up as boys or girls according to taste, and included in the pattern wardrobe are some lovely tiny garments·made from cast-off knitwear. A piece of ribbing is used to make the bright red dress and a pair of short pants for the little black baby. The white baby has a dainty blue romper suit in plain knit, and is wearing a pair of miniature knitted bootees which take only a minute to make from the pattern.

Baby Sue; Baby Boo;
Baby Dee; and Baby Di
 1 = Body × 2
 2 = Head × 2
 3 = Arm × 4
 4 = Shoe × 2
 5 = Fabric dress/smock × 2
 6 = Knitted/baby's dress × 2
 7 = Sleeves for 6 × 2
 8 = Short trousers × 1
 9 = Fabric mob cap × 2
10 = Romper suit × 2
11 = Baby's bonnet × 1

Baby Sue; Baby Boo; Baby Dee; Baby Di

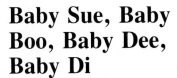

6cm (2¼″)

Baby Sue; Baby Boo; Baby Dee; Baby Di

Cut out the pattern pieces, using the key provided.

To make up the design, follow the general instructions on pages 8–18. Be sure to check any special instructions and techniques used for this pattern. Any extra information is supplied as needed below.

The short trousers, the red dress, the baby's pullover and bonnet are all made from cut-up knitted fabric.

The edges at armhole and neck are turned under and secured with overcast stitches or crochet.

Sew small loops and buttons at the shoulders. For the bootees, use odd scraps of wool.

Cast on 25 stitches, knit for 3cm (1⅛″), cast off 3 stitches on each side, knit 1cm (⅜″) further and fasten off; sew together.

Pattern pieces and hair, dolls left to right (see also page 14 for hair styles):
Mob cap doll: mob cap 9, dress 5, hair *f*.
Black boy: smock 5, trousers 8 (sew together at the crotch with a few stitches), hair *j*.
Baby doll: bonnet 11, pullover 6/7, romper suit 10, shoes 4, hair *a*/*b*.
Pigtail doll: dress 6/7, hair *b*/*d*.
Faces: Eyes 10mm (⅜″) diameter, cheeks 20mm (¾″) diameter, embroider mouths in satin stitch.

Tom Tumble and his sisters

These demure looking charmers are all made from the same basic pattern, and are 22cm (8⅝″) tall. Each pig-tailed doll has a distinct personality. This is achieved by varying details of body fabric, clothes, hair-styles, and small accessories such as lace fabric and ribbon trims. If you are making a doll for a boy, perhaps you could show him Tom Tumble, a bright little clown, with his attractive coordinated outfit. All the clothes are small enough to be made from fabric scraps, and can be sewn in minutes.

Tom Tumble and his sisters

Cut out the pattern pieces, using the key provided.

To make up the design, follow the general instructions on pages 8–18. Be sure to check any special instructions and techniques used for this pattern. Any extra information is supplied as needed below.

To make the body, cut all in one with the legs, from pretty fabric so that it is 'ready dressed'.

It can also be made from two different fabrics by making a seam across the waist.

After stuffing the body fasten the neck to the back of the head and sew on the stuffed arms and shoes.

The clown has no shoes.

The sleeve edges should be trimmed with lace or hemmed before closing the side seams.

Gather them at both ends, draw over the arms and sew to the body.

Faces: Eyes and mouths are 5mm (¼″) diameter; embroider a long stitch across the mouth.

Individual dolls from left to right:

1st doll: Cut the legs as far as the horizontal line on the pattern.

Sew a frill to the pinafore (size including lace 30 × 3.5cm (11¾″ × 1⅝″)).

Make the pinafore yoke and straps from broderie anglaise.

Make the mob cap from two different fabrics: first close the darts, then sew the two pieces together along the curved edges and turn out.

Gather up to fit the head. Make the hair as *b/d* on page 14.

2nd doll: Cut the legs off at the horizontal line on the pattern.

If the body is made from two different fabrics joined together, make the sleeves from the same fabric as the upper body.

Make the short skirt by cutting the pattern at the horizontal line.

Make waistband and straps to fit. Make the hair as *b/d* on page 14.

3rd doll: Cut the legs off at the horizontal line on the pattern.

Make the mob cap as described for the first doll, but in one fabric.

Make hair as *d/m* on page 14. Sew 36cm (14″) lengths of wool along the parting and secure to the head.

Tie around on each side at eye level, then divide into three equal bunches, twist around, coat the ends with a little glue, stick inside the rest of the hair and tie up again.

Clown: Cut out the complete leg pattern with rounded ends.

Make the body, head and arms in white fabric.

Gather up the trousers and sew to the body, then sew on a broad band of doubled fabric, cut to fit.

Sew on a ruff made from broderie anglaise 36 × 4cm (14″ × 1½″).

Make hair as under *g* page 14.

Tom Tumble and Sisters

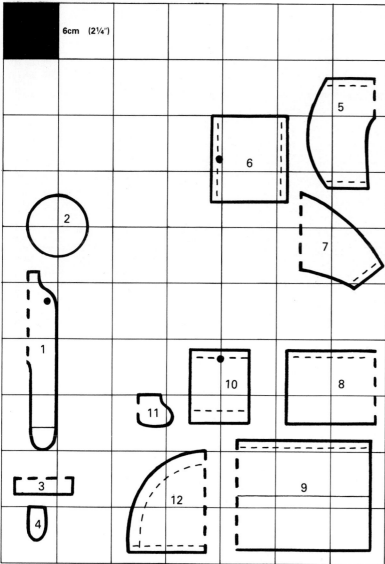

6cm (2¼″)

Tom Tumble and sisters
 1 = Body × 2
 2 = Head × 2
 3 = Arm × 2
 4 = Hand × 4
 5 = Clown's trousers × 2
 6 = Clown's sleeve × 2
 7 = Clown's hat × 1
 8 = Pinafore × 1
 9 = Skirt × 1
10 = Sleeve × 2
11 = Shoe × 2
12 = Mob cap × 2

Magic storybook puppet theatre

Children with active imaginations will love this puppet theatre and its wonderful cast of actors! As long as the wood is pre-cut, the older ones can make the theatre themselves. It is easy to make, and precise instructions are given on how to assemble it. The puppets have soft heads, and represent an archetypal range of goodies and baddies! They can be made either with a long dress and no body or with a short dress and legs. There is another version of the clown on page 50.

Magic Storybook Puppet Theatre

Piano hinge 3 cm (1⅛″) wide × 68 cm (26⅞″) long × 2

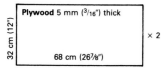

Beading 1.5 × 1.5 cm (⅝″ × ⅝″) × 68 cm (26⅞″) long × 4

Plywood 5 mm (³/₁₆″) thick

32 cm (12″) | 68 cm (26⅞″) | × 2

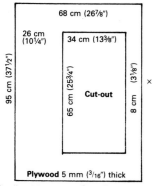

68 cm (26⅞″)

95 cm (37½″) | 26 cm (10¼″) | 34 cm (13⅜″) | 8 cm (3⅛″) | × 1

65 cm (25¾″) | **Cut-out**

Plywood 5 mm (³/₁₆″) thick

Beading 1.5 × 1.5 cm (⅝″ × ⅝″) × 75 cm (29½″) long × 1

Curtain rail 1 cm (⅜″) wide × 75 cm (29½″) long × 1

Magic storybook puppet theatre

Theatre

Cut out the pattern pieces, using the key provided.

Materials: 5mm (¼″) plywood, strips of wood; 2 piano hinges and curtain track to the sizes given in the diagrams. Emulsion paint and polyurethane varnish; cellulose filler; wood glue; 60 × 2cm (¾″) long fine panel pins; 40 × 1.5cm (⅝″) long wood screws; 2 self-adhesive hooks; 20 curtain hooks/runners; 100cm (40″) curtain fabric, 80cm (31½″) wide; 160cm (63½″) curtain tape; 220cm (87″) braid; 100cm (40″) cord; 65cm (25½″) fringing.

To make

Cut out the stage opening to the size shown on the diagram.

Sand the plywood smooth all over and fill any gaps in the edges.

Pin and glue the 68cm (27″) long strips of wood down the sides of the main piece and one edge of each side piece.

Screw the piano hinges onto the strips of the front and side pieces.

Fix the 75cm (29½″) long strip of wood to the inside of the main piece, 5cm (2″) above the stage opening and mount the curtain rail on it.

Paint throughout.

Make up and hang two curtains; draw them back to the sides of the stage opening with the hooks and cord.

Frame the stage opening with braid and fringing.

Puppets

Cut out the pattern pieces, using the key provided.

To make up the design, follow the general instructions on pages 8–18. Be sure to check any special instructions and techniques used for this pattern. Any extra information is supplied as needed below.

Sew the hands to the clothes, then join front to back. Stuff the hands.

Glue a 3cm (1⅛″) long, 2cm (¾″) diameter cardboard or rubber tube into the neck of the stuffed head.

Turn under the neck edge of the clothing, gather up (rather more at the back) and sew onto the neck.

If the figure has legs, a body is also required, but this remains unstuffed.

Set the lightly stuffed trousers or leg pieces (same pattern) onto this.

So that the feet point forward, sew a pleat by hand in the centre front of the trousers.

Secure the body to the neck so that the opening of the neck tube remains accessible behind.

Make noses (no pattern) from felt disks or buttons.

Individual figures from left to right (the descriptions of the hair-styles indicated with small letters are on page 14).

1 Dog Sew legs to the unstuffed body.

2 Policeman Hair *k*, moustache made from strands of wool.

Cut two of the helmet pattern, cut the peak from felt or card without seam allowance and glue on.

3 Burglar Hair and beard *k*. Cut 4 of the cap pattern. Sew the two peak pieces together and top stitch to lower edge of cap.

4 Grandmother Hair: 75cm (29½″) lengths of wool sewn to the centre of the head (*d*). Draw the hair to the back of the head, tie into a loose knot and form into a bun.

5 Gretel Hair *b/d*.

6 Mr. Punch Hair *f*.

7 Princess Hair *d/l*.

8 Devil Cut the hands in one with the dress and the feet with the legs. Sew horns to the head.

Make a braid of wool finished with a tassel and secure to the back. Hair and tail tassel: pieces of fur or bundles of wool.

9 King Hair and beard *k*. The crown is made from gold paper and braid.

10 Variations Additional clothes can be made with back fastenings, so that they can be drawn on over the basic puppet. In this way, for example, the grandmother can serve as a queen or the king as a grandfather.

There are many other possibilities for enlarging the ensemble in this way. The clown on page 50 wears this type of overdress.

11 Animal Glove Puppets Seven different ones are given on page 71.

12 Stuffed Dolls, picture right With the same patterns you can also make stuffed dolls. They have arms, and the neck tube is omitted.

If the clothes are to be taken off, neaten neck and arm edges and provide a fastening at the back.

The two dolls have hair-styles *b/d* (girl) and *f* (boy).

Glove puppets

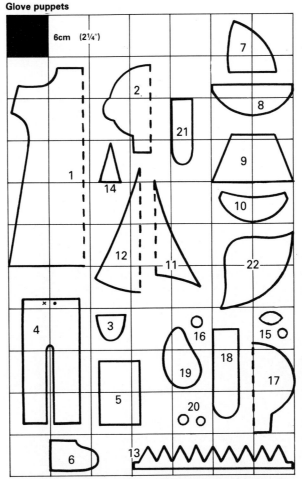

6cm (2¼″)

Glove Puppets

1 = Dress/smock × 2 (shorten as required)
2 = Head × 2
3 = Hand × 4
4 = Leg/trousers × 2
5 = Body × 2
6 = Shoe × 4
7 = Burglar's cap × 4
8 = Burglar's cap peak × 2
9 = Policeman's helmet × 2
10 = Policeman's helmet peak × 1
11 = Clown's hat front × 1
12 = Clown's hat back × 1
13 = King's crown × 1
14 = Devil's horn × 4
15 = Eye × 2
16 = Cheek × 2

Dog

1 = Dress × 2 (shorten)
3 = Hand × 4
5 = Body × 2
17 = Head × 2
18 = Leg × 4
19 = Ear × 4
20 = Eye × 2

Stuffed Dolls

1 = Dress/smock (shorten)
2 = Head × 2
5 = Body × 2
15 = Eye × 2
16 = Cheeks × 2
21 = Arm × 4
22 = Hat × 2

Ten dress-up dolls

Cut out the pattern pieces, using the key provided.

To make up the design, follow the general instructions on pages 8–18. Be sure to check any special instructions and techniques used for this pattern. Any extra information is supplied as needed below.

The numbers indicate the pattern pieces to use, the letters the hair-styles.

For descriptions of how to create the hair-styles see page 14 (woollen hair) and 15 (artificial hair and fur fabric).

Smocks and dresses can be cut down to the length required.

Neck edges are trimmed with lace or bias strips of fabric about 3cm (1⅛″) wide, cut to length required.

Where necessary cut an opening at back neck and neaten.

Dolls on page 34

Faces: Eyes 20mm (¾″) diameter, pupils 15mm (⅝″), cheeks 22mm (⅞″), noses 6–10mm (¼″–⅜″); mouths embroidered.

Clown: Hair *f* (shorten into a fringe at front), smock 7, trousers 11 (long), cap 14. Sew tightly gathered lace to the neck of the smock, 80cm (31½″) long and 4cm (1½″) wide.

Trim sleeve and trouser bottoms with gathered lace.

Black Boy: Hair *h*, using bouclé wool, shirt 10 (fastening at back), trousers 12, shoes 16.

Red Indian: Hair *d*, using wool, shirt 10 (back fastening), trousers 12.

Make felt fringing by cutting halfway across the width of strips of felt.

Sew to neck and bottom edges of smock.

Dolls on page 35

Faces: Eyes 12mm (½″) diameter, cheeks 15mm (⅝″), mouths 10mm (⅜″), finished with satin stitching. Noses about 5mm (¼″) or omit, short socks pattern 13, lengthen to make long ones. Individual dolls, left to right:

1st Doll: Hair *c/d*, in wool, coat 9. Sew loops to right edge of coat and toggle buttons to the right.

Ten Dress-up Dolls

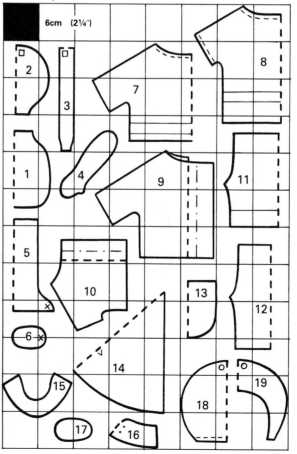

Ten dress-up dolls
1 = Body × 2
2 = Head × 2
3 = Head inset panel × 1
4 = Arm × 4
5 = Leg × 2
6 = Sole × 2
7 = Smock/smock dress × 2
8 = Dress/blouse × 2
9 = Coat × 1 to broken line × 2 to outer edge
10 = Shirt as above
11 = Wide trousers
12 = Narrow trousers × 2
13 = Sock × 2
14 = Clown's cap × 1
15 = Half shoe × 2
16 = Boot × 2
17 = Sole for 15/16 × 2
18 = Wig back × 1
19 = Wig front × 1

For the woolly hat cut up an old glove, sock or pullover cuff; or knit a tube and gather it up at the top.

Make the scarf from a doubled oddment of fabric, shoes 16.

2nd Doll: Hair *c/d* from bouclé wool, dress 8 with a 70 × 5.5cm (27⅝″ × 2⅜″) strip of fabric for the frill.

Gather the neck and add a lace frill. Shoes 15 with laces.

3rd Doll: Bought doll's wig, smock dress 7 trimmed with lace threaded through with ribbon. Shoes 16.

4th Doll: Hair *h* in wool, shirt 10, trousers 12 (long), shoes 16.

5th Doll: Hair *a/d* in wool, blouse 8 (short).

Gather arm and neck edges and trim with lace, then finish the neck edge with a bias strip.

Make the skirt from the border of an old scarf: cut two pieces 42 × 20cm (16½″ × 7⅞″) plus a 25 × 5cm (9¾″ × 2″) band. Shoes 15.

6th Doll: Make the wig from fur fabric with pattern 18/19 (see also under *m*, page 15). Smock 7, with a band sewn to the neck so a cord can be threaded through; trousers 11 (short), shoes 15.

7th Doll: Ready made doll's wig (or make up as under *a/b* or *h*) page 15. Dress 8 with gathered neck finished with a band.

For the pinafore cut a piece of fabric 40 × 10cm (15¾″ × 4″), plus 26 × 6cm (10¼″ × 2¼″) for the waistband and 15 × 3.5cm (6″ × 1⅝″) for each strap; sew as shown in the picture and fasten the waistband at the back with a button. Tie a little kerchief over the head. Shoes, 15 with laces.

Ten dress-up dolls

These dolls show the multitude of variations possible from just one simple pattern! They are all 36cm (14″) high, and depending how they are dressed, they can be boys or girls. By choosing different fabrics, hair-styles and clothes you can create a myriad different personalities. Also, you can sew your doll a complete little wardrobe: a blouse and skirt; shirt or blouse with trousers; play or sleep suit with long or short pants; a smock or nightshirt in varying lengths; a dress, with or without a frill; a useful pinafore; for cold days Dolly will need a warm coat, as well as shoes, socks and hat; underpants and petticoat complete the outfit perfectly! For the first time you will be using a head pattern with an inset panel. This gives extra shape to the head, and recurs in various dolls until page 40, where different head patterns are shown.

Petra and Peter, giant dolls

This sturdy pair of 'giant' dolls are in fact 100cm (39½") tall, but they are still cuddly and friendly to hold. What appeals most to children about these characters is that they are big enough to wear clothes from their young owner's wardrobe. Just the thing to encourage slow dressers to catch up with their doll and get ready fast!

Petra and Peter giant dolls

Cut out the pattern pieces, using the key provided.

To make up the design, follow the general instructions on pages 8–18. Be sure to check any special instructions and techniques used for this pattern. Any extra information is supplied as needed below.

So that they do not become too heavy these large dolls should only be stuffed with soft material (foam chips or man-made fibre filling).

The large flat heads must be tightly stuffed, or soon creases will appear which make the faces look older.

Since the bodies, arms and legs are made from brightly colored fabrics, the dolls appear to be wearing tights and pullovers.

In addition, they can be dressed in pullovers, dresses, jackets, trousers and coats from the children's own wardrobes.

If the dolls are to be given as a present, their first outfit can consist of a dress or pinafore dress made from the pattern, as well as a pullover, or a cheap oddment bought in a sale.

Make the head, hands and ears from flesh-colored fabric (ears for boy only, as the girl's hair covers the area).

The back head pattern could if necessary be cut from a different colored fabric, as it is about three-quarters covered by the wig.

36

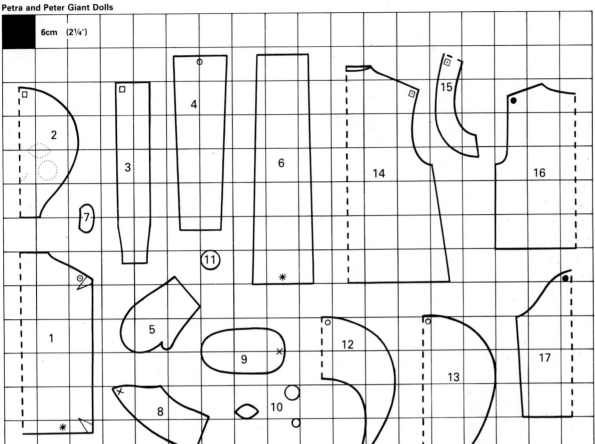

6cm (2¼")

After stuffing put the head into the body, the hands into the arms, the legs into the shoes and sew them all up with invisible stitches.

The nose is a ball button covered with fabric, 2cm (¾") diameter for the boy, 1.5cm (⅝") for the girl.

Hair: The boy in the picture has a short cast-off lady's wig.

He could also have a fur fabric wig like the girl's (made with the pattern, and see under *m*, page 15), or both could have ready-made doll's wigs.

The boy's hair should be designed so that his ears show.

Both dolls also look good with wool hair; suitable styles are *c/d*, or knotted lengths of wool as *i*, or little wool bundles stitched on as *g* and *h* (all on page 14).

Dress: the back and front can either be cut in the normal way from doubled fabric, or pieced together from oddments.

Sew together. Cut an opening at back neck. For a pinafore, cut down centre back and hem narrowly.

Adjust the size of the neck opening by trying the garment on, neaten the edge with a bias strip.

Finish the armholes with facing pieces.

For the skirt frill cut two 80cm (31½") long strips, 8cm (3⅛") wide and join.

Cut the arm frills about 50cm (19¾") long and 5cm (2") wide, hem one side, taper the ends of the other side, gather up and sew to the armholes.

Pullover: Cut this from discarded knitwear, laying the pattern pieces out so that the ends of the main piece, sleeves and collar all meet the edges of the knitwear. (The collar is a 33 × 8cm (12¾" × 3⅛") strip.)

Cut a slit at the back and sew in a zip.

Jimmy the Giant Clown

Make this funny character in fleecy fabric, and he'll be cuddled with glee! Jimmy the Giant Clown is 90cm (35½") from head to toe, and is popular with teenagers as well as younger children. Here his clown costume is made from a fresh gingham check fabric, but you could choose a pattern with spots or stripes – just as traditional.

Jimmy the Giant Clown

Cut out the pattern pieces, using the key provided.

To make up the design, follow the general instructions on pages 8–18. Be sure to check any special instructions and techniques used for this pattern. Any extra information is supplied as needed below.

When cutting out the suit add a 5cm (2") seam allowance at the neck, wrist and ankle edges.

First set the sleeves onto the sides of the suit, then sew pieces and sleeves together. Hem neck, wrist and ankle edges and put elastic through the latter, a cord through the neck.

To make the hat stay on, neaten the bottom edge with bias binding and thread elastic through.

Decorate the suit with two large wound woolly pompons (see page 94).

For hair fix a bundle of wool to each side of the head (see *f*, page 14).

Draw the nose piece up with a gathering thread to 7cm (2¾") diameter and stuff.

If you haven't enough fabric of one pattern to make the suit it can be pieced together from several different ones.

To do this divide the pattern at about waist level, and instead of the fold at centre front and back, make seams.

In the same way the parts of the body hidden by the suit could be made up from oddments (sew hands and feet separately and join up).

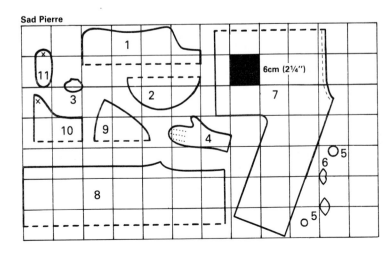

Jimmy the Giant Clown

3.5cm (1⅜")

What are dolls for?

Every child should have at least one cuddly doll or animal to love, to be a very special companion. Dolls mean so many things to their young owners – they are there to provide comfort and security in bed when the world is dark and mother asleep. They are there to be confided in – many children get involved in long conversations with their dolls, also they are there to accept the whole range of childish emotion, from frustration to excited affection. Many people believe that having a doll encourages positive feelings of protectiveness in both little girls and boys, and that this contributes towards making them potentially good parents when they grow up. One thing is certain, having a doll is a crucial part of childhood.

Jimmy the Giant Clown
  1 = Body × 2
  2 = Head × 2
  3 = Head inset panel × 1
  4 = Arm × 4
  5 = Leg × 4
  6 = Ear × 4
  7 = Eye × 2
  8 = Cheek × 2
  9 = Nose × 1
 10 = Suit × 2
 11 = Sleeve × 4
 12 = Pompon × 4
 13 = Hat × 1

Sad Pierre

6cm (2¼")

Sad Pierre
  1 = Body × 2
  2 = Head × 2
  3 = Ear × 4
  4 = Hand × 4
  5 = Eye × 2
  6 = Mouth × 1
  7 = Smock × 2
  8 = Trousers × 2
 10 = Shoe × 2
 11 = Sole × 2

Sad Pierre, Jack and Jill

Pierre, the sad-faced harlequin, will capture the heart of any child. He is 68cm (27″) tall, and has the typical elegant melancholy of the pierrot clowns. His jolly companions have come to visit him at the circus. They are a brother and sister pair, Jack and Jill, each 50cm (19¾″) high. Their heads introduce yet another variation of shaping, this time by using darts.

Jack and Jill

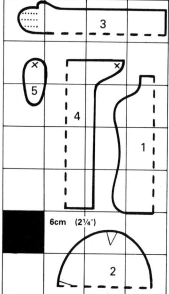

6cm (2¼″)

Jack and Jill

1 = Body × 2
2 = Head × 2
3 = Arm × 2
4 = Leg × 2
5 = Sole × 2

40

Sad Pierre, Jack and Jill

Cut out the pattern pieces, using the key provided.

To make up the design, follow the general instructions on pages 8–18. Be sure to check any special instructions and techniques used for this pattern. Any extra information is supplied as needed below.

As can be seen from the long neck on the body pattern, this is intended to be sewn to the back of the head.

There are no arm and leg patterns as these are made from rolled strips of fabric, as described on page 12.

Sizes: Arms 18cm (7″) long, 3.5cm (1⅜″) diameter. Legs 27cm (10½″) long, 4.2cm (1⅝″) diameter. The ruff is assembled from fabric and lace and measures 110 × 8cm (43½″ × 3⅛″). See also Clowns' Ruffs on page 16.

Hair: *f* or *k* page 14.

Jack and Jill

Making the boy's mop of hair takes a little time, but is worth the trouble as it cannot be damaged and will withstand the most robust handling.

As with the other dolls shown on the following pages, whose heads all have darts, the neck is cut in one with the body, and sewn firmly to the back of the head.

Lines to indicate fingers can be sewn on the hands after stuffing (see girl; the boy's hands are not separated).

As these dolls have the same-size body as those shown on pages 47–50, they can wear all their clothes; all the clothing patterns are on page 51.

The two dolls shown above have hair, clothes and faces as follows:

Girl: Dress 13/14/15 (narrow sleeves), plus a piece 60 × 22cm (23¾" × 8⅝") for the skirt; shoes 20/21; hair a/d, page 14; eyes 12mm (½") diameter; cheeks 25mm (1"), nose 5mm (¼").

Boy: Pullover 6/7; trousers 16; shoes 20/21; hair *i*, page 14; eyes 15mm (⅝") diameter, cheeks 32mm (1³⁄₁₆"), nose 12mm (½").

National Costume dolls

Cut out the pattern pieces, using the key provided.

To make up the design, follow the general instructions on pages 8–18. Be sure to check any special instructions and techniques used for this pattern. Any extra information is supplied as needed below.

All the heads can be made in two different ways. Either use felt fabric in a flesh color, or a piece of knitted cotton, 20cm (7⅞") diameter, drawn together at the edge with gathering threads (back view as E in photograph on page 48).

The neck is fastened to the back of the head and must then also be covered.

National Costume dolls

One of the most popular hobbies of doll lovers, whatever age they may be, is collecting dolls in national costume. They are really not intended to be used as playthings, but as decorative treasures. The collection includes a Japanese girl; a Russian boy; a Dutch girl; a Turkish boy; and finally a Bavarian boy and girl. Also, from the same pattern you can make the beautiful period dolls pictured on page 44, and the doll shown on page 57 (centre top). These have the same heads and bodies, and their patterns are included in the diagram on page 43. In this set of dolls you will learn a new way of making noses with balls which can lie over or under the skin. On the Turkish boy and the Japanese girl they are omitted. Depending on the length of the legs, the dolls range from 39–44cm (15⅜"– 17¼") high.

Arms, legs and hands should also be made in the same fabric, depending on whether they are disguised by clothes or not.

The patterns for the body pieces are in square I, those for the clothing in squares II to IX.

Faces: Eyes 12mm (½″) diameter, with an arch embroidered above in stem stitch; mouth 8mm (¼″) diameter with satin stitch embroidered across it (or use satin stitch only).

The legs are with or without feet, depending on the shoes. When shoes are separate, stuff the tips firmly and insert the straight leg pieces, 4A.

The slits necessary for pulling a garment on, shown in squares II, VI, VII, VIII are closed by hand.

For button closing add an overlap piece to each side of the pattern.

42

Individual dolls are described left to right.

The roman numbers indicate the square containing the clothing patterns. The descriptions of the hair styles, indicated by small letters, are on page 14 for wool hair, on page 15 for artificial hair:

Japanese Girl (picture page 41)

Pattern IV, hair *a/b* from bought doll's hair. Leg B, length 2. Embroider the eyelines slantwise.

Kimono: sew front to back at shoulders.

Sew sleeves along side 1 to mark; leave side 2 open. Sew the sleeve seam from 3 to 4 and close the kimono side seams.

Turn front facing to inside, narrowing hem arm edges 2 and 5.

Finish the neck opening with a 32 × 4cm (12½″ ×

1½") bias strip of fabric.

Put the kimono on, encircle the upper body with ribbon and sew on at the back.

Russian Boy (picture page 41)

Pattern V, hair style *k/n* in wool. Legs A, length 1.

Cut out one of the hat pattern in fur fabric and sew together, first at the back and then on top.

Dutch Girl (picture page 41)

Pattern VI, hair style *a* in bought doll's hair. Legs A, length 1.

Sew the clogs from pattern in felt, or buy tiny wooden ones.

Cut two of the bonnet, sew along sides 1 and 2, turn out, then join down centre back.

Cut out an 80 × 19cm (63½" × 7½") skirt, and 18 × 11cm (7" × 4¼") apron (plus lace trim 5cm (2") deep) with waistband 50 × 3.5cm (19¾" × 1⅜").

Turkish Boy (picture page 42)

Pattern VII, hair *a/b* (short) from bought doll's hair.

Legs A, length 1.

Cover head, neck, hands and legs with brown knitted cotton.

Glue slightly larger white felt disks under the eyes.

Turban: cut out a 13.5cm (5¼") diameter piece of fabric and a strip 23 × 11cm (9" × 4¼").

Gather the circular piece around the edge and sew to the top of the head.

Fold the strip in half lengthwise and sew into a band; sew its centre to the back of the head.

Cross the ends in front, tuck in at the back and sew down.

Bolero: cut out with a seam allowance at shoulders only.

Sew the shoes together along side 1, then set in the soles.

Bavarian Boy and Girl (picture page 42)

Girl: Pattern VIII, hair *a/b* in hemp. Legs B, length 1, shoes as for Sailor Boy (III).

Cut out a 45 × 16cm (18" × 6¼") skirt, 15 × 15cm (6" × 6") apron with 50 × 3.5cm (19¾" × 1⅜") waistband.

National Costume dolls (also Bertie, and Lily, 44 Charity, 57)

I
1 =	Body × 2
2 =	Head × 2
3 =	Arm × 4
4A =	Leg without foot × 2
4B =	Leg with foot × 2

II
5 =	Dress × 2
6 =	Hatbrim × 1
7 =	Boot × 2

III
8 =	Blouse front × 2
9 =	Blouse back × 1
10 =	Collar × 2
11 =	Hat × 2
12 =	Trousers × 2
13 =	Lace-up shoe × 2
14 =	Sole × 2

IV
15 =	Kimono front × 2
16 =	Kimono back × 1
17 =	Sleeve × 2
18 =	Shoe × 2
19 =	Sole × 2

V
20 =	Smock × 2
21 =	Hat × 1
22 =	Trousers × 2
23 =	Boot × 2
24 =	Sole × 2

VI
25 =	Dress top × 2
26 =	Bonnet × 2
27 =	Shoe × 2
28 =	Sole × 2

VII
29 =	Trousers × 2
30 =	Shirt × 2
31 =	Bolero × 1
32 =	Shoe × 2
33 =	Sole × 2

VIII
34 =	Bodice × 1
35 =	Blouse × 2

IX
36 =	Shirt back × 1
37 =	Shirt front × 2
38 =	Collar × 1
39 =	Jacket back × 1
40 =	Jacket front × 2
41 =	Trousers × 2
42 =	Fly × 1
43 =	Hat × 2

National Costume Dolls Bertie and Lily, 44, Charity, 57

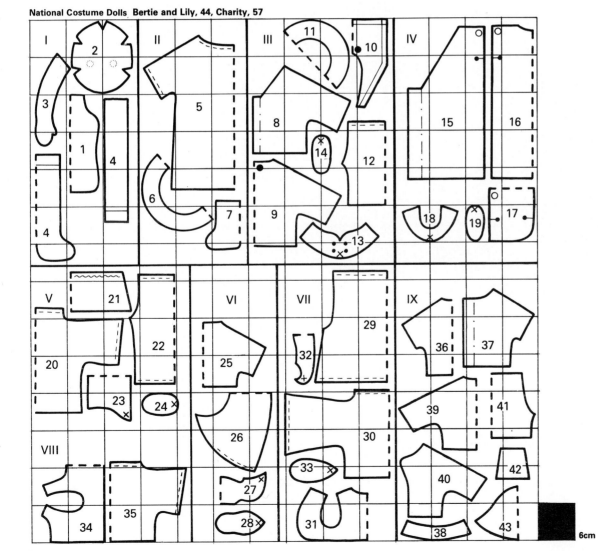

6cm (2¼")

This jaunty 'Edwardian' sailor and his lady fair evoke nostalgic sighs for a far off time. They are made from the same pattern as the national dress series on pages 41–42. Again, they are collectors' dolls, and are not meant to be routine toys. They would make a wonderful gift for adults who like dolls, as well as children. As with the other collector's dolls in this book, you will enjoy making the accurately detailed costumes, which provide an authentic period touch.

The bodice (open at back) is made in felt so only needs a seam allowance at shoulders and waist.

Boy: Pattern IX, hair *g* in hemp. Legs B, length 1. Shoes as for Sailor Boy (III).

Sew up the flap-style fly for the trousers and secure with two buttons at the top.

Turn the jacket revers outwards and indicate button holes with satin stitches. Make decorative braces (suspenders) from braid.

Sew flat shoe laces or strips of felt 5mm (t″) wide onto the neck, jacket fronts and sleeve bottoms.

The point of the hat should be pushed in.

Bertie and Lily: Edwardian dolls

Lily

Pattern II, hair *a/b/d* from bought doll's hair. Legs A, length 2.

Make the dress in length 2 from white fabric, add the 4cm (1½″) white lace trimming and then dye.

For the felt hat see page 18. Cut the brim from the pattern, and make the crown from a 12cm (4¾″) diameter felt circle moulded over an 8cm (3⅛″) diameter jar.

Sew shoes on firmly.

Bertie

Pattern III, hair *g* from bought hair. Legs B, length 2.

Victorian dolls: Thomas and Sarah

This beautiful pair of collectors' dolls really express the finer points of the craft of toymaking. They are 56cm (22") high, and have a quaint Victorian air – as if a little girl and boy of bygone days were sitting all dressed up in their best clothes all set to go to a special party. Their garments are exquisitely designed, and would look best in velvet and lace trimming for a luxurious touch. Artificial hair provides a realistic effect, and here for the first time you can try some basic modelling. The nose is shaped from under the skin, as described in detail on page 12.

Sew the collar, trimmed with narrow ribbon (line 2) turn and sew to neck opening of blouse.

Make up a band from a strip of fabric 36 × 4cm (14″ × 1½″) and tie around under the collar.

Sew the 7 × 7 (2¾″ × 2¾″) knitted dicky to the body.
Sailor hat: cut 2, then remove a circle from the inside of one piece (line 1); sew outer edges together.

Cut out a fabric strip 27.5 × 5cm (10¾″ × 2″), sew ribbon down one half, fold and sew the strip into a band and close into a circle.

Sew to edge 1 of the hat.

Victorian Dolls, Thomas and Sarah

Cut out the pattern pieces, using the key provided.

To make up the design, follow the general instructions on pages 8–18. Be sure to check any special instructions and techniques used for this pattern. Any extra information is supplied as needed below.

The patterns above are also used for Arabella and Oliver shown on pages 55 and 57.

Pieces 3A, 3B, 9A, 9B and 16 are not needed for Thomas and Sarah; also the body, line 1, and length 2 on pieces 10 and 11, do not apply.

The neck, cut in one with the body, is sewn to the back of the head.

The neck cover is secured on top; put a little stuffing in at the same time.

As described on page 13, the 1.5cm (⅝″) long cone-shaped nose is pushed in from the forehead.

The 12cm (4¾″) long rolled fabric arms, 3cm (1⅛″) in diameter, are put into the stuffed hands (3C).

The 28cm (11″) long leg rolls, 3.5cm (1⅜″) in diameter, are put into the feet, stuffed at the tips. (For making fabric roll limbs see page 12.)

Mouth and eyes can be painted straight on if the fabric is smooth enough; otherwise make them up separately on non-fraying fabric and glue on.

Create them following the instructions and drawings on page 54; both dolls have eyes size D and mouth E, with a long stitch embroidered across the mouth.

Sarah: Use a bought doll's wig, or make up according to *a, h* or *l* on page 15.

Make the dress bodice to length 1 and cut out a 70 × 30cm (27⅝ × 11¾″) skirt.

Cut the white dress front to size required on double fabric, sew and turn out; trim with broderie anglaise.

Finish the neck with a white bias strip.

Thomas: Use a bought doll's wig or make up according to *g* or *l* on page 15 and glue on.

Gather the trouser bottoms and set a 14 × 4cm (5½″ × 1½″) strip onto the right side; turn under and stitch lightly to the wrong side.

Sew darts in jacket back, gather the fronts along the neck edges to fit.

Make up the collar and trim with lace.

Sew on after turning in the front facing.

Thomas and Sarah, (also Arabella, 55; Hope, 57)

 1 = Body × 2
 2 = Head × 2
 3 = Hand × 4
 4 = Foot × 2
 5 = Ear × 4
 6 = Neck cover × 1
 7 = Trousers/pants × 2
 8 = Sleeve × 2
9A = Upper sleeve × 2
9B = Lower sleeve × 2
10 = Dress bodice front × 2
11 = Dress bodice back × 1
12 = Jacket front × 2
13 = Jacket back × 1
14 = Jacket collar × 2
15 = Lace-up shoe × 2
16 = Boot × 2
17 = Shoe with straps × 2
18 = Soles for 15/16/17

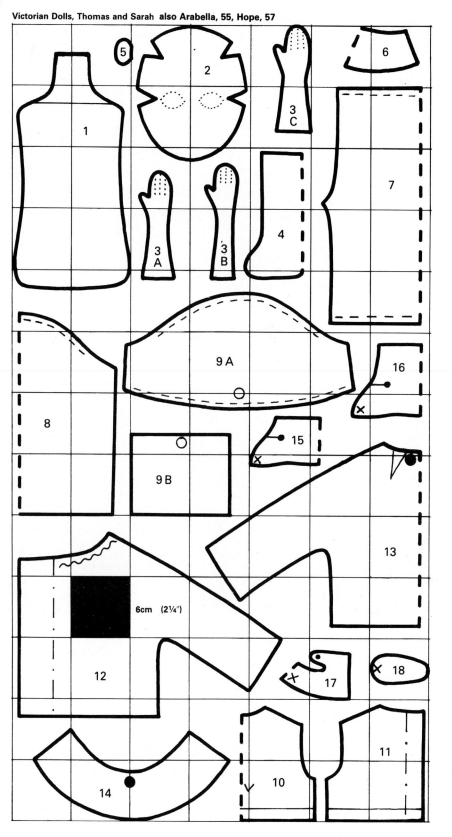

Polly and Patsy with their families

These endearing doll families provide a good opportunity to learn how to make modelled fabric heads and bodies. They are 50–55cm (19¾″–21¾″) tall, and their soft, beautifully shaped bodies make them very lifelike. This is further enhanced by the appealing expressions produced by modelling the heads and arranging the features. For example, the way you position the nose strongly influences the face – if you place it high up it produces a snub-nosed 'babyish' effect. Lower down, it makes the face look older. The two baby dolls (4th from the left in the top picture, and 1st from the left below) are made from a separate pattern on page 49. Instructions for making up are also on that page. All the other dolls are made from the pattern on page 48, and their clothes are cut from the new set of patterns on page 51.

Polly and Patsy with their families
(pictures page 47)

Cut out the pattern pieces, using the key provided.

To make up the design, follow the general instructions on pages 8–18. Be sure to check any special instructions and techniques used for this pattern. Any extra information is supplied as needed below.

Heads: These are all made the same way. Sew the two head pieces together, stuff from above, draw the opening together and bind around about 1cm (⅜″) above the centre. (See photograph, right.)

The nose is placed at about the centre of the face; use pattern to cut out a circle, gather and stuff (B); alternatively, sew on a small wooden ball.

Draw the cheek disks up to measure 3.5cm (1⅜″) diameter, stuff and sew to the face about 3cm (1⅛″) apart (A and C).

Then pull on the head covering piece (D), made from a fine, soft fabric and sew together at the back (E).

Next put on the second covering piece (F), in flesh-colored fabric, which is cut on the same pattern as D but should be 5mm (¼″) larger all around.

On the line of the binding around the head make the eye sockets with two satin stitches, about 10mm (⅜″) wide: stab stitch right through the head and draw the threads tight at back (G).

If felt eyes are to be used it is advisable to equalize and smooth out these 'eye holes' by spreading on several layers of glue (allow to dry thoroughly in between each layer).

If button eyes are to be sewn on this is not necessary.

The eyes are 10mm (⅜″) in diameter; mouths can be glued on, or embroidered with satin stitches.

When sewing on eye buttons and embroidering mouths sew right through to the back of the head.

The finished body (H) is sewn firmly to the back of the head (on about the lower third).

Over this comes the circular rear head piece (I), with stuffing placed beneath it.

It can be made of the same fabric as the head, or to match the color of the hair.

If the doll is to have a wig made according to a pattern, or bought ready-made, this rear head piece is not needed.

Arms and Legs

These are all made the same way.

Fabric rolls are made up in the following dimensions (K, see also page 12). Arms 3.4cm (1⅜″) diameter, length 15cm (6″); legs 4.4cm (1¾″) diameter, length as required.

They are covered with knitted cotton or a tube of fabric and set into the ready-stuffed hands and feet.

The hand pattern has two outlines: the longer hands are for dolls that look relatively older.

Also choose the leg length according to the apparent age of the doll.

Clothing, Hair and Leg Lengths (clothing patterns on page 51). Also refer to general instructions pages 16–18.

Page 47, top picture, left to right

1st Doll (Polly): Leg length 26cm (10¼″). Dress 13/14/15

48

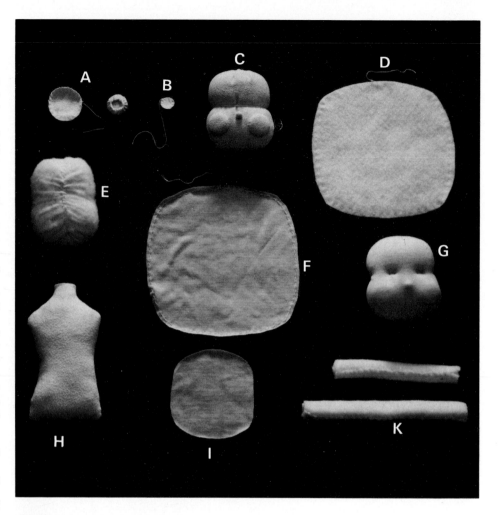

Polly and Patsy with their Families

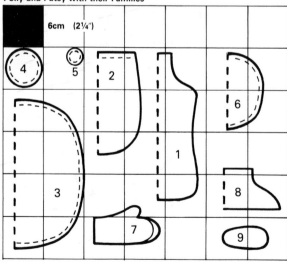

Polly and Patsy

1 = Body × 2
2 = Head × 2
3 = Head cover × 1
4 = Cheek × 2
5 = Nose × 1
6 = Rear head piece × 1
7 = Hand × 4
8 = Foot × 2
9 = Sole × 2

(wider sleeve), 80 × 33cm (31¼″ × 12⅞″) piece for skirt, shoes 19, hair a/b in hemp (page 15).
2nd Doll: Leg length 19cm (7½″), cut head without seam allowance.

Dress 13/14/15 (wider sleeves); piece for skirt 80 × 23cm (31¼″ × 9″), and for frilly collar 25 × 4cm (9¾″ × 1½″).

Pinafore yoke 17, plus skirt piece 75 × 14cm (29½″ × 5½″).

Socks 10, shoes 19, hair a/b (page 15) in hemp (tinted).
3rd Doll: Leg length 22cm (8⅝″), smock 1 in length 1, with sleeve length as required.

Sew a band made from a 27.5 × 3.5cm (10⅞″ × 1⅜″) bias strip of fabric to the neck edge and thread a drawstring through.

Trousers 16, shoes 18, ready-made doll's wig.
Baby doll: See this page.

Page 47, lower picture, left to right
Baby Doll: See this page.
2nd Doll: Leg length 23cm (9″). Smock 1 in length 1, neck band as for 3rd doll above, trousers 16 (short), socks 10, shoes 20, hair c/d/e in wool (page 14).
3rd Doll: Leg length 22cm (8⅝″). Dress 1, 1 in length 2, neck band as for 3rd doll above, socks 10 (lengthen), shoes 19, hair c/d/e in wool (page 14).
4th Doll (Patsy): Leg length 22cm (8⅝″), pullover 6/7 (made from cast-off knitwear).

Cut a 13.5 × 4cm (5¼″ × 1½″) strip for the polo neck. Jacket 12, allowing 3.5cm (1⅜″) on the sleeves as a cuff – turn to the inside and sew down, then turn back to the outside.

Skirt 54 × 18cm (21¼″ × 7″), waistband 27 × 5.5cm (10½″ × 2⅛″). Socks 10 (lengthen by 3cm (1⅛″)), shoes 19, hair a bought doll's wig or c d e in wool (page 14).

Materials
Be careful to choose the right fabric for making these finely featured dolls. For the 'skin' knitted cotton or fine jersey is best, also the sort of knitted rayon which is used for undies. In fact any fine, flexible fabric will do. Save this fabric for covering visible parts such as the head, hands, arms and legs. The rest of the body can be made up in another fabric if necessary. For the inner head covering (piece D) and the arm and leg rolls, use fleecy textured soft, thick fabric for the best results.

Baby dolls (pictures on page 47 and 50, see captions)

Cut out the pattern pieces, using the key provided.

To make up the design, follow the general instructions on pages 8–18. Be sure to check any special instructions and techniques used for this pattern. Any extra information is supplied as needed below.

All three baby dolls are made with the same pattern. The head is made as described on page 48.

The patterns for the head covering, cheeks and nose are also there.

They have hair and clothing made as follows:
Picture page 47 above right: Make the wig from fur fabric using the pattern, and a jacket with wide sleeves (outer line).

Cut the back down through the centre.
Picture page 47 below left: Use a doll's wig or make up as in g on page 15.

Make the jacket with narrow sleeves and cut down through centre back.

Make smock with short sleeves (inner, faint line).
Picture page 50 below (Baby Jane): Hair g, page 14, dress with long sleeves.

The tights are the same for all these dolls, also the faces.
Faces: Eyes are 8mm (¼″) diameter, mouths 10mm (⅜″) diameter, embroidered straight across with satin stitch.

By lengthening the dress pattern a christening robe can be made also.

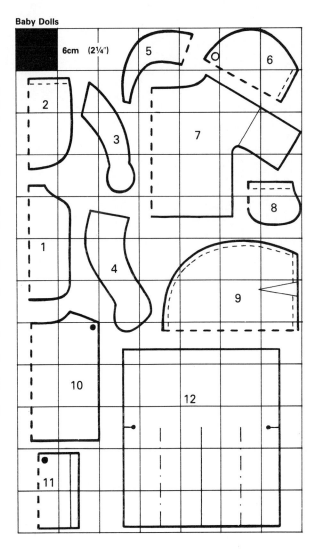

Baby Dolls

6cm (2¼″)

Baby dolls (47, 50)
1 = Body × 2
2 = Head × 2
3 = Arm × 4
4 = Leg × 4
5 = Wig front × 1
6 = Wig back × 1
7 = Dress/Smock × 2
8 = Shoe × 2
9 = Mob cap × 1
10 = Jacket × 2
11 = Jacket sleeve × 2
12 = Tights × 1

Simon, Rosie and Baby Jane

This merry trio is joined by a small doll and a glove puppet who have already appeared on pages 38 and 32. The two larger dolls, Simon and Rosie, are made from the same pattern as those on page 47, while Baby Jane is made from the same pattern as the other baby dolls also included in the picture on page 47. The pattern for Baby Jane appears on page 49. The clothes shown in the pattern on page 51 are also meant to be worn by Simon and Rosie. These dolls are extra examples of the modelled fabric variety.

Simon, Rosie and Baby Jane

Rosie (with flowered dress): Leg length 22cm (8⅝″). Dress 13/14/15 (wider sleeves), plus a 60 × 23cm (23½″ × 9″) skirt, 120 × 5cm (47⅜″ × 2″) skirt frill and 25 × 4cm (9¾″ × 1½″) frill.

Socks 10 (lengthen), shoes 19, hair *c/d/e* in wool (page 14).

Simon (with knitted jacket): Leg length 22cm (8⅝″). lover 6/7 (made from cast-off knitwear) with a strip 13.5 × 3.5cm (5⅜″ × 1⅜″) for the polo neck.

Trousers 16, jacket knit 3/4/5 in garter stitch (all knit), and knit on a band at the neck.

Socks 10, shoes 18, sew on fur fabric wig (see also under *m* on page 15).

Baby doll (Jane). See page 49.

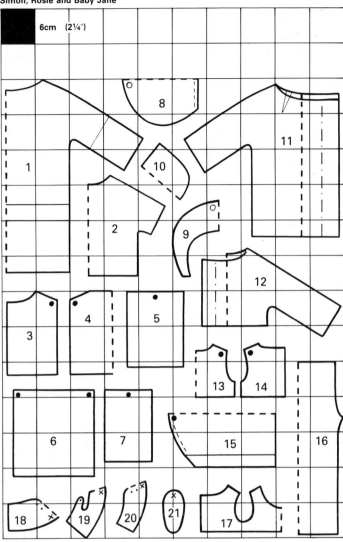

6cm (2¼")

Doll's Clothes

1 = Smock/dress/ nightshirt/pyjama top × 2

2 = Blouse × 2

3 = Knitted jacket front × 2

4 = Knitted jacket back × 1

5 = Knitted jacket sleeve × 2

6 = Pullover × 2

7 = Pullover sleeve × 2

8 = Wig back × 1

9 = Wig front × 1

10 = Sock × 2

11 = Coat × 1 to broken line
　　　　× 2 to outer edge

12 = Jacket × 1 to broken line
　　　　× 2 to outer edge

13 = Dress front × 1

14 = Dress back × 2

15 = Dress sleeve × 2

16 = Trousers/pants × 2

17 = Pinafore/dress yoke × 2
(1 of these in lining fabric)

18 = Boot × 2

19 = Shoe with straps × 2

20 = Lace-up shoe × 2

21 = Soles for 18/19/20

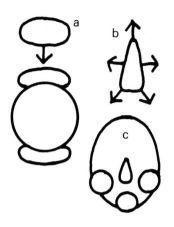

Clay modelling

The next series of dolls include those with modelled clay heads and limbs. Clay modelling is not difficult, especially since you can use self-hardening clay, which is very easy to handle. Depending on how skilful you are, you can make heads, hands and shoes which are either simple or elaborate. If you do decide to make one of the clay modelled dolls you must remember to set aside a few evenings to complete the job – this is not a hobby for those with extremely limited time.

Equipment

You do not need a great amount of equipment to model clay heads and limbs. You will need: a rolling pin; coarse and fine sandpaper; orange sticks; a flexible nail file; a wood rasp; a kitchen knife and a knitting needle. Artist's modelling sticks, available in a range of sizes, will also be useful, but they are not absolutely vital. Once you have made one of these beautiful clay modelled dolls, you can take pride in the knowledge that you have produced a unique creation with your own hands.

Clay modelling

A number of different modelling materials are available from art stores, handicraft shops or department stores.

They should always be used according to the manufacturer's instructions.

Here we show dolls with heads and limbs made from a self-hardening modelling material which, after suitable treatment of the surface, has a ceramic-like appearance.

This material is very easy to use, and can be shaped as required by adding layers or sanding down, filing and carving.

The shaped pieces and layers added later (these must always go on to a damp base) are modelled immediately, in their soft condition, and smoothed with a damp finger.

Final smoothing down and any carving necessary follow when the material is dry. Leftover material can be used up if it is stored in an airtight plastic box, or wrapped in aluminium foil, so that it remains soft.

Heads with Busts

For sizes see also page 9. So that the head is not too heavy it has a core consisting of a polystyrene or cellulose ball.

With a rolling pin, roll the modelling clay out to about 6mm (¼″) thick for a small head, 8mm (⅜″) thick for a large one.

Dampen the ball and roll the clay around it.

By adding a disk of clay above and below and moulding all three together the ball is turned into an oval (diagram a).

The neck consists of a short roll of clay, the bust of a slab about 3mm (⅛″) thick and as wide as the head, rounded off at the corners.

For large dolls make the bust to the width of the shoulders.

The bust is bent to the shape of the body (this is made up without a neck) and according to its size should have 4–6 holes made in it with a knitting needle so that it can be sewn in place.

After leaving the head, neck and bust pieces (picture II, page 53) to dry for several hours dampen their joining surfaces, roughen them with the point of a knife and join them together.

For extra strength a cut-down knitting needle or wooden dowel can be inserted through the neck.

This is recommended on large heads but is not necessary on small ones. The needle should pierce the head and bust, and can also continue for a few centimetres into the body.

If there has been a long break in the work and the parts have dried out, they can be joined with contact glue.

To cover the joins between them use little rolls of clay, about 5mm (¼″) thick, and spread it out thinly, adding more as necessary, to form a smooth transition from head to neck and from neck to bust.

The additional modelling which may be carried out can be seen in pictures II–IV on page 53.

After finishing the head leave it for several days to dry, then smooth the head with sandpaper, the nose area with a fine rasp.

Now eyes and mouths can be tried out in soft pencil (do not press) or cut-out features arranged, and wigs tried on.

This will help you judge whether the head looks right and if necessary improve it, to a more pleasing shape.

After a final careful smoothing down remove all the sanding dust and paint the head.

Use a soft, flat paintbrush and water-based paint, in skin color (white with a little brown and red added) in two thin coats.

Paint on the face and varnish if required. (See also page 54.)

Text for heads illustrated on page 53 above

I Here we see the individual pieces which make up the basic shape of every head: oval shape, neck, bust and nose.

II To make a nose, first model a cone (see picture).

Set this onto the centre of the face and, where it joins, spread it out carefully with an orange stick or modelling tool in the direction of the arrows (diagram b).

This simple face shape can be created quite successfully by a beginner at the first attempt, and can be used for both dolls and clowns.

Gaston on page 55 has this type of head, plus ears.

These can be omitted on dolls' heads by using more hair, if making them presents difficulties.

III This head can be made by beginners too.

After covering the ball, press eye sockets into the still-soft clay just above the centre of the face with two index fingers (not too deeply).

Take care they are level, and that enough space remains between them for the nose.

After leaving to dry add the nose as under II.

The heads of Arabella (page 55) and Hope (page 57) are made this way, and you can see from them that even with this simple modelling really beautiful dolls can be created.

IV This head is worked further and requires a little experience of modelling.

Because of the virtually endless possibilities the material offers for correcting and improving, however, even beginners can achieve quite satisfying results given a little patience.

After making the head as under III above leave it to dry for a few hours.

Then shape three little balls of clay for cheeks and chin and put them on the face (diagram c).

Smooth them down until no joins can be seen.

In addition, any head can have a mouth moulded on, made from little rolls of clay. Only the very experienced should attempt this however.

Hands, Lower Arms and Shoes, picture page 53 (below)

As a guide to the size required use the drawing of the part given on the diagram-pattern.

A Take two equal-sized rolls of clay, thicker at one end than the other, and flatten the thin ends with the fingertips.

Modelled heads

Each of the three heads above are examples of various ways of using modelling clay with different degrees of complexity. The finished heads can be seen on the following dolls:
II *Clown, page 55;* **III** *Doll, page 55 left and Doll page 57 right;* **IV** *Doll page 55 centre. The picture below shows how a fabric arm is fixed to a modelled hand. Proceed in the same way for fixing modelled feet to fabric legs.*

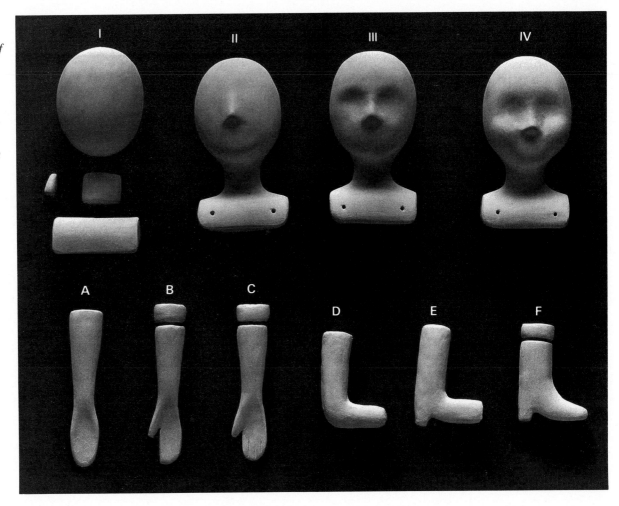

B Cut out a wedge with a pointed knife and score a groove for fixing the arm in place using a knitting needle.
C Form the thumb and score finger lines. Provided that the hand is still soft you can also bend it into a gentle curve.

Forming individual fingers is only possible on large dolls. To do this, instead of scoring the hand as shown in the picture cut it very carefully into three with a knife.
D For shoes make two identical rolls and bend each into a right angle.
E Cut out a wedge and form the heel.
F Smooth a little more clay onto the instep and score a groove round the top.

After smoothing down paint the hands the same color as the face, the shoes in brown or black. For boots paint on laces. Finish the hands with matt varnish like the head, or polish. Shoes, if not painted with gloss, should be gloss varnished.

Securing to the Body

Arms and Legs or Shoes
Make up tubes from strips of fabric, to the dimensions given in the instructions for individual dolls. Turn a small hem under at one end and gather up.

Slip this end onto the groove in the finished arm, leg or shoe. Draw the gathering thread up tight so that the tube is drawn securely into the groove (picture G left). In addition, the end of the arm or leg can be smeared with a little glue before fixing.
Now stuff arms and legs lightly.
Take the legs in at the knee by hand.
Sew the limbs firmly to the well-stuffed body.
The stitches will be hidden by the clothing.

Head with Bust
Sew the bust tightly to the body with strong doubled thread. If the pre-bored holes do not give enough grip, further ones can be made with a fine wood drill.

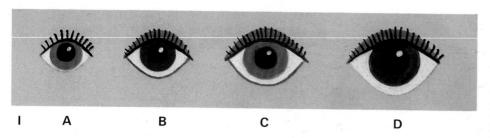

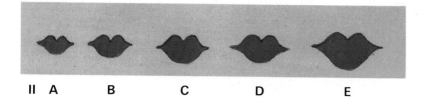

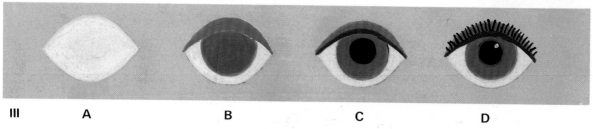

I Actual size eyes
II Actual size mouths
III Painting sequence
These drawings show the methods used for painting on features, whether on modelled, wooden or fabric heads. If you are painting on fabric, you must first check to make sure that the surface is very smooth. Also, if the fabric is colored, make sure that the dye is fast (test a small piece). If the fabric is not suitable for direct painting, then paint eyes and mouths on a non-fraying fabric (such as the kind used for interfacings), cut them out and glue them onto the head. Examples of this technique are shown on the dolls on page 45, and the clown on page 55. If you choose this method, you can embroider eyelashes on separately with fine black thread. This also helps to secure the eyes in position. Embroider shorter eyelashes below the eye. You can also secure a glued-on mouth with a line of satin stitches, sewn firmly into the head fabric.

Painting the Faces

Suitable paints are acrylics, poster paints and water colors. If inexperienced it is advisable to practise first on paper.

Eyes: Draw the iris as a complete circle, which is then covered at the top by the eyelid. It can be blue, brown, grey, green or any mixture required.

The white highlight at the edge of the black pupil gives the eyes a lively appearance. High-quality artist's paint brushes are essential for success.

Paint the edge of the eyelid, eyelashes and mouth outline with a very fine brush.

Do the highlight and the remaining parts with a thicker brush.

Eyelashes can also be made with a drawing pen and Indian ink.

Allow each color used to dry thoroughly before applying the next color. Eyebrows can be added if required, in light to mid-brown; or omitted.

For the mouth mix some white and a very little brown into red paint.

Alternatively use nail varnish in a brownish-red shade.

Paint or spray the painted heads with colorless matt varnish. Also polish with a soft cloth to give a gentle sheen. (It is important that paint and varnish are compatible; check when buying, or carry out a test.)

54

Text for above pictures

IA Draw the outline in pencil (see also IIIA) and paint the eye white.

Then paint the iris, pupil, highlight, eyelid and eyelashes, in that order. B, C, D are made in exactly the same way. They are simply bigger.

II A-E First draw a horizontal line in pencil, then mark the centre of the mouth.

Starting at the centre draw the upper lip, then the lower.

III **A** First pencil a horizontal guide line from one corner of the eye to the other, and a vertical line down the centre.

Use these to draw the outline; the upper curve is slightly higher than the lower. Paint white.

B Paint the eyelid light brown and the iris as required.

C Paint the eyelid edge black or brown, the pupil black.

D Make a white dot for highlight, holding the brush vertically and well loaded with paint.

Paint black eyelashes; if painting directly onto the face they can be continued above the eyelid

In addition you can paint the lower edge of the eye with a fine light brown line; or in black for a clown (see picture I).

Arabella, Mary and Gaston

These examples of dolls with modelled heads and limbs inspire you to emulate such gorgeous creations. They are purely for decoration of course, and are ideal models for the sumptuous costumes shown in the picture. Gaston is yet another in the series of clowns in this book, and he wears the traditional 'white-face' clown make-up. His glowing silken clothes and splendid ruff make him an elegant gift. Both Arabella and Mary will also be welcomed by a lucky owner. They each have finely made dresses, full petticoats trimmed with lace or frills, and lace trimmed drawers which are meant to peep out from beneath the dresses.

Mary
1 = Body × 2
2 = Hand × 2 (modelled)
3 = Boot × 2 (modelled)
4 = Dress × 1

Gaston
1 = Body × 2
2 = Hand × 2 (modelled)
3 = Leg/shoe × 2 (modelled)
4 = Smock × 1
5 = Trousers × 2
6 = Hat × 2
7 = Ear × 2 (modelled)

Mary

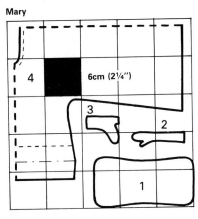

6cm (2¼")

4
3
2
1

Gaston

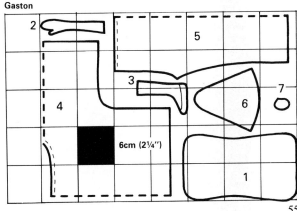

2
5
3
4
6
7
1
6cm (2¼")

Arabella, Mary and Gaston (picture page 55)

Cut out the pattern pieces, using the key provided.

To make up the design, follow the general instructions on pages 8–18. Be sure to check any special instructions and techniques used for this pattern. Any extra information is supplied as needed below.

Arabella: left hand of picture. Height 56cm (22"). The patterns for the body, hands and clothing are on page 46. As these dolls are the same size as the ones described there and illustrated on page 47, the heads and clothing are interchangeable.

So, for example, Thomas and Sarah on page 45 could have clay heads instead of fabric ones.

Head and hands are modelled and fastened on as described on pages 52–54, with head III, finished height 11cm (4¼"), diameter of internal ball about 7cm (2¾").

Use the following patterns from page 46: Body 1 to line 1 (without neck), hands 3B as a reference for modelling, dress bodice 10/11 in length 2, sleeves 9A and 9B, boots 16/18.

For the skirt cut a piece of fabric 80 × 33cm (31½" × 12⅞"), for the arms cut two strips 12 × 8cm (4¾" × 3⅛"), for legs make two rolls 28cm long by 3.5cm (11" × 1⅜") diameter (see page 12) and put into the boots, stuffed at the bottom. Make the hair following a/c on page 15; paint eyes and mouth C from page 54.

Mary: Centre of picture. Height 46cm (18"). The pattern is on page 55, left. Head, hands and shoes are modelled as described on pages 52–54, using head IV, with a finished height of 7.5cm (3"), inner ball diameter about 5cm (2").

The fabric strips for the arms measure 9 × 6.5cm (3½" × 2½"), for the legs 16 × 7.5cm (6¼" × 3"). The skirt frill measures 100 × 8cm (40" × 3⅛"), the neck frill 40 × 4.5cm (15¾" × 1¾").

The skirt of the dress will fall into even folds if gathered up at waist level with two rows of running stitches about 1cm (⅜") apart.

The wig is made as h or i on page 15.

Paint eyes and mouth B, page 54.

Gaston: Right of picture. Height 52cm (20½"). The pattern is on page 55. Head, hands and legs are modelled as described on pages 52–54 using head II with a finished height of 9cm (3½"); internal ball diameter about 6cm (2¼").

Follow pattern pieces 2, 3 and 7 when making the hands, legs and ears, then paint the body parts white and the shoes black.

For the arms cut fabric strips 10 × 7cm (4" × 2¾"), for the legs 16 × 8cm (6¼" × 3⅛").

The large ruff is made from two pieces, each 150 × 8cm (59¼" × 3⅛") (including lace). The hair is made in style i, page 15.

Paint eyes C and mouth D as on page 54.

Oliver, Charity, Faith and Hope (picture page 57)

Cut out the pattern pieces, using the key provided.

To make up the design, follow the general instructions on pages 8–18. Be sure to check any special instructions and techniques used for this pattern. Any extra information is supplied as needed below.

Oliver

The shaped head is created by darts, and a cone-shaped nose, 2cm (¾") long, pushed underneath the skin (see page 13); it is also shaped by very careful stuffing.

As described on page 54, paint the eyes (D) and mouth (E) separately, cut them out and glue on.

Embroider on the eye make-up lines and a horizontal line across the mouth with a few satin stitches, the eyebrows with stem stitch.

For arms make up 19cm (7½") long fabric rolls, 3cm (1⅛") in diameter; for the legs rolls 26cm (10¼") long and 3.5cm (1⅜") diameter (see page 12).

The smock frill is 140 × 7cm (55⅜" × 2¾"), the ruff two pieces of curtain voile, 150 × 11cm (59¼" × 4¼").

The smock is decorated with two 3cm (1⅛") diameter woolly pompons (for how to make see page 94).

The shoes have velvet bows. The hair is in style i, page 15.

Charity (large centre doll)

This doll belongs to the series shown on pages 41 and 42, National Costume dolls. It is made with the same pattern, see page 44 in squares I, II and III.

Use legs A, length 2, dress length 1, boots 7.

For the skirt frill cut a piece 75 × 15cm (29¼" × 6").

Crochet the hat as described on page 18 and make the hair in style a/c on page 15.

The eyes are 12mm (½") diameter, the mouth 8mm (¼").

Oliver

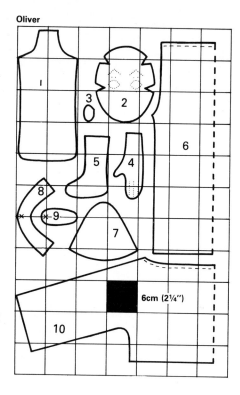

Oliver

1 = Body × 2
2 = Head × 2
3 = Ear × 4
4 = Hand × 4
5 = Leg × 4
6 = Trousers × 2
7 = Hat × 2
8 = Shoe × 2
9 = Sole × 2
10 = Smock × 2

6cm (2¼")

Oliver, Charity, Faith and Hope

This exquisite group of collectors' dolls represents a mixed bag of modelling methods. Oliver, the handsome pierrot, is made from fabric and his head is shaped in the same way as the dolls on page 45, with a nose cone placed beneath the skin. He is 68cm (27″) tall. Charity, the larger doll at the back, belongs to the series of dolls shown on pages 41 and 42, and is made with the same pattern. Faith, the smaller doll in the front, has a body frame made from wired rope, a new method which is fully described on page 61. Only Hope has a clay modelled head, and she is made in the same way as Arabella on page 55. She wears a very glamorous bought wig, and is 56cm (22″) tall.

Embroider an arch of stem stitches over the eyes and a satin stitch across the mouth.

Faith (small centre doll)

This doll has a wired-rope skeleton with a head made from a wooden ball, and is made exactly like the three dolls described and illustrated on pages 61–62.

The pattern is on page 61: you will need pieces 1, 2, 4 and 10 from the diagram pattern.

The skirt is 50 × 17cm (35½″ × 3½″), the waistband 16 × 5cm (6″ × 2″).

The felt hat is described on page 18. Make the wig in style *k*, page 15.

Hope (right-hand doll)

This 56cm (22″) high doll is especially beautiful, with a touch of nostalgia.

She has a modelled head and is made just like Arabella on page 55 left – see instructions for modelling on pages 52–54.

Her distinguishing feature is the bought wig; but this could equally be made up using style *a/c*, *h* or *l* on page 15.

Her dress has a frill at the top made from a 65 × 6cm (25¾″ × 2¼″) strip of fabric and sleeves made from pattern 8, page 46.

Tina and Tonto

*Tina and Tonto are easy to
make and great fun to play
with. You can bend them into
any position that you can think
of, because they are made from
a 'skeleton' of wire-stiffened
sisal rope. These dolls should
only be given to older children
and teenagers, since there is a
possibility that babies might
expose the wire in some way.
Tina and Tonto are wearing
bright, simple outfits which
allow plenty of movement –
you could easily make up one
of these dolls into a very
athletic footballer for devoted
fans! They are both 30cm
(11¾″) tall, and have heads
made from bought head balls.*

Tina and Tonto

Cut out the pattern pieces, using the key provided.

To make up the design, follow the general instructions
on pages 8–18. Be sure to check any special instructions
and techniques used for this pattern. Any extra information is supplied as needed below.

The heads have a diameter of 5cm (2″). For Tonto,
the head, neck, hands and feet are wound around with
dampened reddish-brown raffia.

Spread the head and rope first with a little glue.

The clothing patterns are the same for both figures.
The blouse or smock has a slit in the back, which is
glued together after pulling it on.

Before sewing up trousers, glue felt strips to sides.

Cut these into a fringe when finished.

The head band and lower smock edge are also decorated with felt; gaily colored feathers complete the head
dress.

For hair-styles see page 15. The eyes are felt disks
4mm (⅛″) diameter, the mouth a 4mm (⅛″) disk, glued
in place.

Many other original figures can be made with these
basic patterns. The blouse pattern can be lengthened to
make dresses, and these can be decorated in all sorts of
ways.

Alternatively set on a gathered skirt at waist level.

In the same way many different dolls with the most
varied wardrobes can join the group.

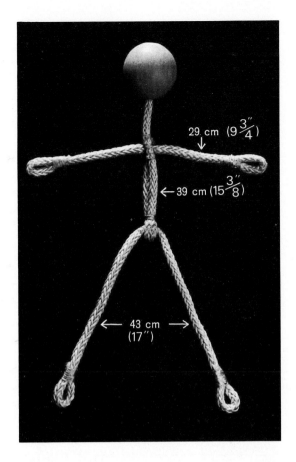

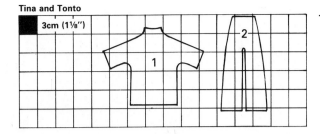

Tina and Tonto

3cm (1⅛")

1

2

Tina and Tonto
1 = Blouse/smock × 2
2 = Trousers × 2

Jenny and Joey the Clown

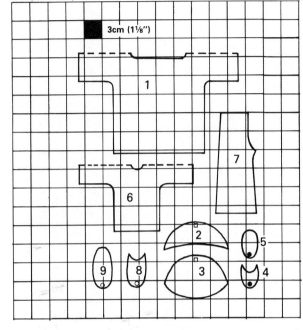

3cm (1⅛")

1

6

7

2

3

9

8

5

4

Jenny and Joey
1 = Dress × 1
2 = Wig front × 1
3 = Wig back × 1
4 = Upper shoe × 2
4 = Sole × 2
6 = Shirt × 1
7 = Trousers × 4
8 = Upper shoe × 2
9 = Sole × 2

29 cm (9¾")

39 cm (15⅜")

43 cm (17")

Wired-rope Skeleton I

1. Cut the pieces of rope, which can be up to 8mm (¼") in diameter, to the sizes given, using pliers to get through the wire core.

2. Bend as shown and secure by winding around with strong thread.

3 Stick the arms and legs through the body loop, bind together where they cross and secure with a few stitches.

4. Bore a hole in the wood, cellulose or polystyrene head ball (unless it already has one).

5. Coat the neck end of the rope with glue and push it in. (With polystyrene balls use special polystyrene glue, or natural latex adhesive; other types may dissolve it.

Jenny and Joey the Clown

Here are two more delightful wired rope dolls, this time a little girl called Jenny, hand in hand with Joey the Clown. You can just imagine him running about in the circus, throwing custard pies and water over everyone! This pair are much more solid in appearance than the previous wired rope dolls, because they have larger heads and shorter necks.

As mentioned before, these dolls are never given to young children or babies because wire is used in their make-up. Even for older children, we recommend that the ends of the wire must be tightly bound with thread and glue. For a final safety precaution, the ends should then be covered with strong sticky tape. If you have no fur scraps, both dolls could have practically any wig on pages 14 and 15.

Jenny and Joey the Clown

Cut out the pattern pieces, using the key provided.

To make up the design, follow the general instructions on pages 8–18. Be sure to check any special instructions and techniques used for this pattern. Any extra information is supplied as needed below.

These are made with the same rope skeleton as before, but the neck is stuck further into the head, which should have a diameter of about 8cm (3⅛″).

The skeleton is wrapped around with cotton wool, held in place by winding thread around it.

Head, neck, body and limbs are covered with pieces cut from old socks, or with knitted cotton.

The head cover needs a diameter of 16cm (6¼″) and is drawn up with a gathering thread (the back view of this is shown in picture E on page 48).

For arms and legs sew tubes.

Hair: Jenny has a wig made with the pattern from scraps of fur or fur fabric (see also under *m*, page 15).

Joey's hair is made from a strip of fur fabric as *j*, page 15.

A circle of hair made from lengths of wool would suit him equally well (see *k*, page 14).

Faces: Jenny's eye disks are 10/14mm (⅜″ × ⅝″) diameter, her mouth is a heart shape, rounded off the point (lower lip).

For Joey the diameter of the eyes is 8mm (⅜″), the cheeks 12mm (½″), nose 16mm (⅝″).

For the mouth glue on a piece of yarn or felt.

Wired-rope Skeleton II

This is basically the same as the one on page 59, but without the bent-back hands and feet, and it has a body made with a pattern put on top.

The assembly of the rope can be seen from the picture.

Cut the rope lengths (up to 8mm (⅜″) diameter) to the lengths shown, snipping the wire with pliers.

Stick the arms and legs through the rope body, which is doubled just up to where the arms join on, and bound around, then sew them securely where they cross.

Spread glue on the neck and stick it into the head, which will need a hole bored in it if none exists.

If using an egg shape instead of a ball, place the neck in it slightly behind the centre (see picture).

The finished skeleton should be laid between two fabric body pieces.

Sew these together by hand and stuff.

Bind the arms and legs with cotton wool, thick fleecy fabric or scraps of wool, just thickly enough for the hands and clothing to fit comfortably over them.

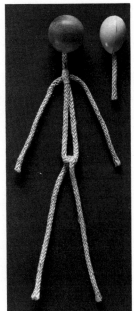

Cowboy Tex, Alice and Calico (picture page 62)

Cut out the pattern pieces, using the key provided.

To make up the design, follow the general instructions on pages 8–18. Be sure to check any special instructions and techniques used for this pattern. Any extra information is supplied as needed below.

All three rope figures have skeleton II.

The head diameters are 6cm (2¼″), with eyes and mouths painted as IA and IIB respectively, see page 54.

The legs are put into the shoes, stuffed at the bottom.

The long drawers for the female figures can be made with the cowboy pants pattern cut to the required width and length.

Alice (left-hand doll): Cut a skirt 50 × 18cm (19¾″ × 7″), plus strip for upper frill 40 × 5cm (15¾″ × 2″), skirt frill 90 × 7cm (35½″ × 2¾″).

Crochet the hat following the instructions on page 18.

Make the hair as a/c page 15.

Calico (centre doll): Cut a 50 × 27cm (19¾″ × 10½″) skirt, 18 × 14cm (7″ × 5½″) apron with a 55 x 3.5cm (21¾″ × 1⅜″) waistband.

Cut the scarf with pattern 15.

Make the hat with brim from pattern 11, as described on page 18.

Prepare colored hemp hair (see page 15) and a hairstyle like that for the grandmother on page 63.

Cowboy Tex: Cut the shirt down centre front, turn the edges under and after putting on glue together.

Also glue on the cuffs.

Make the waistcoat from chamois leather and glue on a leather belt after fitting the trousers.

Hat: After sewing the two hat pieces sew on the brim.

Glue on hair as j (or i, k or l page 15).

Paint on eyes, without eyebrows or eyelashes, and a mouth rather thinner than B.

Cowboy Tex, Alice and Calico Grannie and Grandpa

Tex, Alice and Calico
1 = Body × 2
2 = Hand × 4
3 = Blouse/shirt × 1
4 = Dress bodice × 1
5 = Trousers/pants × 2
6 = Doll's shoe × 2
7 = Cowboy's shoe × 2
8 = Cowboy's hat × 2
9 = Cowboy's hat brim × 1
10 = Doll's hat brim × 1
11 = Doll's hat brim × 1
12 = Bolero back × 1
13 = Bolero front × 2
14 = Cowboy's neckerchief × 1
15 = Eliza's scarf × 1

Grandparents
1 = Body × 2
2 = Hand × 4
15 = Scarf × 1
16 = Dress × 1
17 = House jacket × 1
18 = Dicky × 1
19 = Trousers × 2
20 = Waistcoat × 1
21 = Apron × 1
22 = Slipper × 2
23 = Sole × 2

6cm (2¼″)

Cowboy Tex, Alice and Calico

Cowboy Tex and his ladies may belong right back in the last century on the Western frontier of America. Alternatively, Alice and Calico could well come straight from a Victorian household in London! Wherever they belong in your imagination, they make beautiful, decorative dolls, and stand 45cm (18") tall. They have the same bodies, heads and skeletons as the Grandmother and Grandfather dolls described in the next pattern. They differ from the usual wired rope dolls because they have proper bodies. Faith, the doll on page 57 with a wired rope frame, is also made from this same pattern.

Grannie and Grandpa (picture page 63)

Cut out the pattern pieces, using the key provided.

To make up the design, follow the general instructions on pages 8–18. Be sure to check any special instructions and techniques used for this pattern. Any extra information is supplied as needed below.

This pair, with the same wired-rope skeleton, bodies and hands as the wooden-headed dolls shown on page 62, have handmade cotton wool heads (see picture above), 7cm (2¾") in diameter.

For how to make the skeletons see page 61 and the picture above.

The diameter for the head covering is 14cm (5½"), for the eyes 3mm (⅛"), for the nose ball 7mm (¼").

When embroidering the mouths with satin stitch, draw the thread right through to the back of the head and pull it tight, so that the mouth is slightly sunken.

Glue bits of wool on for the eyebrows or embroider them in stem stitch.

The legs/feet, covered with thick socks, should be bent forward by 4cm (1½") in the front and inserted into the felt slippers.

The hands, sewn from the same fabric as the head covering, are drawn over the arm rope.

Grandmother: For the hair sew 30cm (11¾") lengths of wool into a strip as shown in picture *d* on page 14.

Lay the strands over the side of the head, cross over at the back, pile up on top and glue in place.

Knit the shawl in darning wool, in garter stitch (all knit).

Start with 100 stitches and decrease by two stitches at the beginning of each row.

For her knitting, knit across 18 stitches for 3cm (1⅛"), then put the stitches onto toothpicks.

Grannie and Grandpa

This venerable pair sit together cosily on their own little couch, which is easy to make from the pattern provided. They are made from the same pattern as the dolls on the previous page. With their snowy white hair and eyebrows, and beautifully detailed clothes, they project an air of wisdom and serenity which is very soothing. Any child who has a special relationship with Grannie and Grandpa will welcome this unusual 'set piece' grouping.

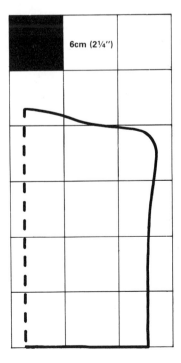

6cm (2¼")

Grandfather: Hair in style *k*, page 14; for the beard sew on a small bundle of wool.

Glue on the dicky and wing collar cut from 2cm (¾") wide strips of felt; sew on the bow tie.

Put on the felt waistcoat after sewing the trousers.

The jacket edges should be finished with braid, cut without seam allowance.

Sofa

Cut the back rest according to the pattern from thick cardboard or hardboard.

Glue some plastic foam about 4mm (⅛") thick over it, or up to three layers of thick fabric.

From the same pattern but adding a 12mm (½") seam allowance cut two covers and sew together with a ½cm (¼") seam (leave open at the bottom).

Draw over the back, then fold the lower edges to the inside and sew together by hand.

The 28 × 9 × 9cm (11″ × 3½″ × 3½″) seat consists of plastic foam (use several layers) or a block of wood.

Cut the covering material for the seat 50 × 25cm (19¾″ × 9¾″), and two pieces 14 × 10cm (5½″ × 4″) for the arms.

Cover the seat.

After sewing up the arm covers draw up one end with a gathering thread, stuff and then sew up the other end from outside.

Glue the backrest and arms to the seat and also secure with invisible stitches.

Three felt mascots

The blackbird, ladybird and mouse shown here are made from scraps of felt, and are each about the size of the palm of your hand. They are simplicity itself to cut out (no need for extra seam allowances with felt). The running stitches act as a decorative feature.

3 felt mascots
1 = Body × 2
2 = Wing × 2
3 = Paw × 2
4 = Foot × 2
5 = Head × 1
6 = Ear × 2
7 = Beak × 1
8 = Tail × 2
9 = Cheek × 2
10 = Tooth × 2
11 = Spot × 8
12 = Eye × 2

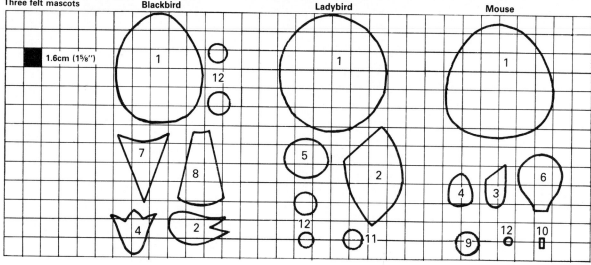

Three felt mascots   Blackbird   Ladybird   Mouse

1.6cm (1⅝″)

Three felt mascots

To make up the design, follow the general instructions on pages 8–18. Be sure to check any special instructions and techniques used for this pattern. Any extra information is supplied as needed below.

The basic pattern is an oval. The blackbird has a tail, sewn onto the back to make him stand up.

Legs, wings and the double beak pieces are simply glued on firmly where they join.

On the mouse, include the ears and paws when sewing around the body; glue on the feet after stuffing and sew on a ball button nose. Fix a braided wool tail to the back.

As shown in the photograph, the ladybird has sewn-on wings. She also has two braided raffia feelers, and six little legs made from short lengths of raffia, which are pulled through the edges of the body and knotted in place.

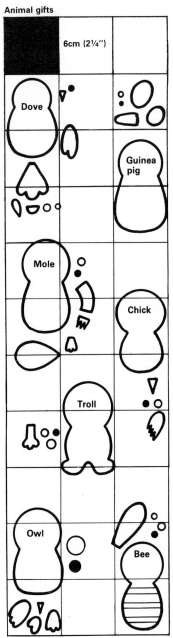

Animal gifts		
	6cm (2¼")	
Dove		Guinea pig
Mole		Chick
	Troll	
Owl		Bee

Animal gifts

Here are seven little gifts to make up in felt or any other fabric scraps you have lying around in your workbag. These patterns make up into figures about 10cm (4") high. You can choose from a troll, a chick, a dove, a mole (centre), an owl, a bee and a guinea pig.

Animal gifts

To make up the design, follow the general instructions on pages 8–18. Be sure to check any special instructions and techniques used for this pattern. Any extra information is supplied as needed below.

The smaller pieces in these patterns have not been labelled, as it can be seen from the photograph what they are.

Simply cut two of each body piece, sew together and stuff. All other parts consist of just a single piece of felt, except for the mole's arms, which consist of two pieces glued together, so that the white claws can be sandwiched between them.

All features and other parts are glued on. The troll

and the mole have buttons for noses.

Glue the bee's brown stripes in place before sewing the body.

Woollen loops are sewn to the head of the red troll; make a stitch to secure after every loop.

For the legs of the chick and bee pull 13cm (5") lengths of wool or yarn through the body and braid them together. The bee's feelers are made the same way from shorter pieces.

Draw lengths of thread through the black mole's face and glue them in place where they emerge.

The owl's ears are loops of wool.

More animal gifts

These 'quick make' creatures can be made from a wide variety of fabric and trimmings. Since they are meant for babies, you should choose bright colors, and fabrics that are easy to wash. If the baby is teething you might even make up the pattern in a plastic coated fabric. Use little pieces of braid, wool and ribbon to trim. The patterns shown here are for a mouse, a bird, a pony, a bear, a duckling and a fish.

More animal gifts

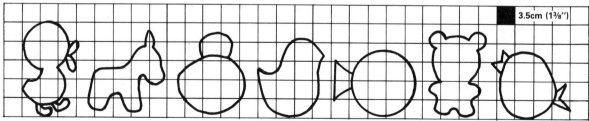

3.5cm (1⅜")

More animal gifts

To make up the design, follow the general instructions on pages 8–18. Be sure to check any special instructions and techniques used for this pattern. Any extra information is supplied as needed below.

These little animals are easily made, as you can see from the photograph. Cut two of each piece, adding a seam allowance of 2mm (1/16") for those made in plastic coated fabric, and 5mm (¼") for those made in towelling.

Separate parts to be sewn on later – like the duck's feet, fish fins, bird's tail and beak – should include a 1.5cm (⅝") allowance along the joining edges.

Troll-squash; Piggy-squash; Doggy-squash

Here are some super animal cushion toys, in the shape of a troll, a piglet and a dog. They are about 40cm (15¾″) in height, and are very popular with teenagers as well as younger folk. In fact grown-ups like them too! You'll often see them riding in the car. Use all your imagination to combine some interesting fabrics, and you're sure to come up with the jolliest creatures ever.

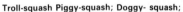

Troll-squash Piggy-squash; Doggy- squash;

3.4cm (1⅜″)

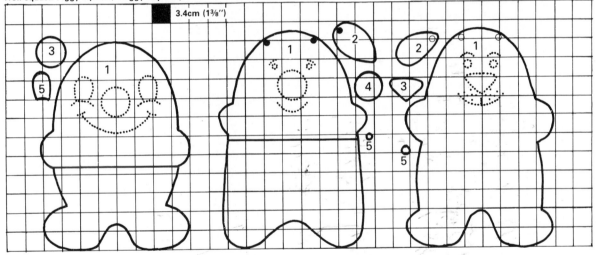

Animal cushions
1 = Body × 2
2 = Ear × 4
3 = Nose × 1
4 = Pig snout × 1
5 = Eye × 2

Apply any braid or ric-rac before sewing pieces together; similarly glue wool or yarn loops to the wrong side of the pieces before sewing together.

Animals made from plastic coated fabric are sewn together by hand, wrong sides facing; those made from towelling are sewn right sides together and turned out.

Troll-squash; Piggy-squash; and Doggy-squash

To make up the design, follow the general instructions on pages 8–18. Be sure to check any special instructions and techniques used for this pattern. Any extra information is supplied as needed below.

With bi-colored figures first join upper and lower bodies, then sew these together.

Make shoulder straps from strips of fabric or braid, sewn on at centre back and fastened in front as shown.

For hair the troll has three bundles of 12cm (4¾″) lengths of raffia, sewn on (see page 14). Don't overstuff, these should be usable as cushions.
Fabric: dog, 42 × 65cm (16½″ × 25¾″); piglet, 22 × 65cm (8⅝″ × 25¾″) in pink and the same quantity in blue; troll, 25 × 62cm (9¾″ × 24½″) in red and 18 × 60cm (7″ × 23¾″) in tartan check.

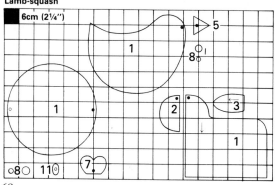

Bird-squash; Fish-squash; Lamb-squash

Here (far left) is another collection of cuddly animal cushions – these are cut out in profile shapes. The patterns make up into a bird, a fish and a lamb. Any brightly colored fabrics can be used for the bird and the fish. If you are making the lamb, however, do try to get a fleecy fabric as similar as possible to a real lamb's coat.

Growly Bear; Moo the Calf; Bow-wow the Dog

These funny cushion 'faces' on the left make charming little toy pets, and are made up here in a variety of fleecy and furry fabrics. Each one of them can be attached to the body shape described opposite, and hey presto! you have a unique animal bed rug.

Bird-squash; Fish-squash; Lamb-squash

6cm (2¼")

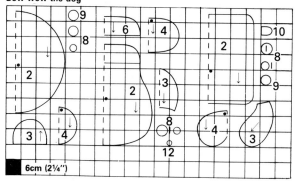

Growly bear; Moo the calf; Bow-wow the dog

6cm (2¼")

Animal cushions
1 = Body × 2
2 = Head × 2
3 = Ear × 4
4 = Muzzle × 1
5 = Beak × 2
6 = Forehead × 1
7 = Tail fin × 2
8 = Eye × 2
9 = Nose × 1
10 = Tongue × 1
11 = Mouth × 2
12 = Nostril × 2

Bird-squash; fish-squash; lamb-squash

To make up the design, follow the general instructions on pages 8–18. Be sure to check any special instructions and techniques used for this pattern. Any extra information is supplied as needed below.

Here are three more snuggly animal cushions to make.

Bird

The outline of the bird's 36cm (14″) body is not much harder to draw than that for the round fish.

The beak should be turned out, lightly stuffed and attached while sewing the body pieces together.

Fabric: 35 × 80cm (13¾″ × 31½″) for the body; a scrap of yellow for the beak.

Fish

The 35cm (13¾″) diameter fish is made from the simplest of shapes, namely two circles; these can be made up from two or more different fabrics.

The tail is turned out, lightly stuffed and included while sewing together the body; the mouth is set onto the front.

Fabric: 23 × 80cm (9″ × 31½″) patterned, 20 × 80cm (7⅞″ × 31½″) plain.

Lamb

The cuddly, 41cm (16″) long lamb is also made with an easy-to-copy pattern.

Sew the face pieces to the body pieces, then sew the figure together.

Make up the ears and sew on.

The eyes consist of a curved line of stem stitches with satin stitches radiating from it.

Fabric: 40 × 70cm (15¾″ × 27½″) for the body; 20 × 30cm (7⅞″ × 11¾″) for face and inner ears.

Growly Bear; Moo the Calf; Bow-wow the Dog

To make up the design, follow the general instructions on pages 8–18. Be sure to check any special instructions and techniques used for this pattern. Any extra information is supplied as needed below.

Bear's head

This cushion, 37cm (14½″) across, again uses a simple round shape, this time giving a front view. The muzzle should be sewn on by hand and lightly stuffed.

Fabric: 45 × 100cm (18″ × 39½″), plus 35 × 20cm (13¾″ × 7⅞″) for muzzle and ear linings.

Calf's head

For the front of the 36cm (14″) wide calf cut a separate piece in fur fabric, indicated by the straight line across the pattern, to make the forehead, and join the two.

Cut the rear piece all in one. Make up the ears and set them on the sides.

Sew the muzzle on by hand, inserting a little stuffing in it.

Fabric: 42 × 100cm (16½″ × 39½″); 65 × 16cm (25¾″ × 6¼″) for muzzle and ear linings; an oddment of fur fabric for the forehead, 32 × 10cm (12¼″ × 4″).

Dog's head

This time the head is made with a 36 × 35cm (14″ × 13¾″) piece, gently rounded off at the corners.

As before the muzzle is sewn on by hand and lightly stuffed.

Fabric: 30 × 105cm (11¾″ × 41½″); 26 × 16cm (10¼″ × 6¼″) for the muzzle; 26 × 22cm (10¼″ × 8⅝″) for the ear linings.

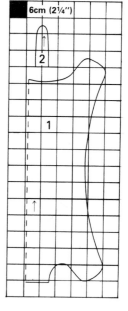

Bed rug
1 = Body × 2
2 = Tail × 2

Bed rug

To make up the design, follow the general instructions on pages 8–18. Be sure to check any special instructions and techniques used for this pattern. Any extra information is supplied as needed below.

All three of the cushions shown on page 68, or similar heads of your own design, can be attached to a flat body piece so as to make a bed rug.

If using a bear's head simply shorten the tail a little; for a calf rug, substitute a twisted woollen cord with a tassel.

Fasten the neck part of the body to the back of the head cushion. You can also lightly stuff the body, or insert a sheet of foam.

If required the body pattern can be enlarged a little, by cutting it across the middle and inserting a panel.

Fabric: body, 90 × 60cm (35½″ × 23¾″); lining 85 × 60cm (33½″ × 23½″); for the head see under bear's, calf's or dog's head.

Animal glove puppets

Remember the puppet theatre on page 32? As well as the puppets shown there you could also play with these wonderful characters – a piglet, a rabbit, a frog in the top picture, and a fox, a goose, a hedgehog and a sealion below. You can make two kinds of glove puppets, either open at the bottom, or with legs. Those with legs have slits to fit over the hand. If you wish you can stuff all the puppets to make cuddly toys, and they are also useful as gift wraps for presents which can be tucked in the body.

Glove puppets
1 = Body × 2
2 = Head × 2
3 = Head inset panel × 1
4 = Beak × 4
5 = Muzzle × 1
6 = Ear × 4
7 = Pig snout × 1
8 = Cheek × 2
9 = Nose × 1
10 = Eye × 2

Animal glove puppets

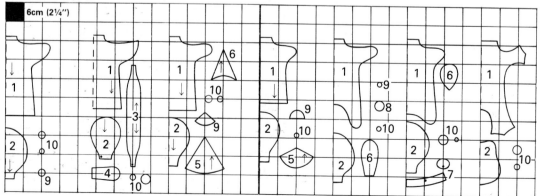

6cm (2¼")

The picture (left) shows the variations possible by stuffing the puppets to make soft toys. Also, they can be made up in less 'realistic' looking fabrics. Shown here is a view of a frog with a back opening – this is needed for those puppets made with legs. The fingers go through the slit and into the 'arms' in order to manipulate the puppets freely.

Animal glove puppets

To make up the design, follow the general instructions on pages 8–18. Be sure to check any special instructions and techniques used for this pattern. Any extra information is supplied as needed below.

Piglet

This can be made with legs, or left open at the bottom like the figures below. Figures which are open and intended to be used as puppets need a tube of cardboard slipped into the neck opening. After stuffing the head, take a 2cm (¾″) tube, 3cm (1⅛″) long, and glue it into the neck opening. Turn the neck edge over, and insert the head. Stitch firmly in place with invisible stitches. The frog does not have a tube.

Sew the oval snout piece to the narrow curved one, stuff and sew the finished snout onto the face.

Cheeks and eyes are embroidered as described on page 12.

Fabric: 75 × 40cm (29½″ × 15¾″) towelling.

Rabbit

Like the piglet, this can have a body with or without legs.

Make up the ears and sew on; make the nose from a fabric button.

Filled with chocolate eggs, he becomes an ideal Easter gift.

Fabric: 70 × 40cm (27½″ × 15¾″) towelling.

Frog

With this glove puppet the fingers only reach into the arms, not into the head as with the other animals, so no cardboard tube is required.

Sew the body to the back of the head (see the picture on page 71 showing the back view).

Fabric: 75 × 40cm (29½″ × 15¾″) felt.

Fox

Place the long muzzle on the face with the seam running down the centre, underneath, and place the nose on top, made up in the same way.

To finish, draw three pieces of thread, stiffened with wax, through the muzzle and secure by knotting them close to it.

Fabric: 40 × 70cm (15¾″ × 27½″) felt.

Goose

This head differs from the other in this series in that it is in profile, with a centre panel between the two head pieces.

The beak pieces are turned out and stiffened with cardboard.

Fabric: 35 × 75cm (13¾″ × 29½″) furry fabric plus an oddment for the beak.

Hedgehog

Knot 12cm (4¾″) lengths of wool or raffia along the seam line of the finished head (see page 14).

A single row is enough to indicate the prickles, but if you have time the whole head and also the back can be covered.

Place the muzzle on the head so the seam faces down, and position the nose similarly on top.

Fabric: 27 × 70cm (10½″ × 27½″). Fleecy fabric.

Sealion

Make the beard from a band of 8cm (3⅛″) lengths of black wool, about 2.5cm (1″) wide, sewn together in the centre. Fold the band in the middle and sew it to the face so that the wool strands point downwards, just above the nose button.

Fabric: 42 × 70cm (16½″ × 27½″) fleecy fabric.

Henrietta Hen and chicks

This colorful feathered family would make a really lovely present at Easter. We chose the sunniest colored fabrics we could find, in this case the fabric is easy-to-wash towelling. The mother hen has been made up from several pieces of different patterns, and has a smart ric-rac braid trim.

Chicken

1 = Body × 2
2 = Head × 2
3 = Body inset panel × 1
4 = Wing × 4
5 = Tail × 2
6 = Muzzle × 2
7 = Comb × 2
8 = Eye × 2

Chicks

1 = Body × 2
2 = Body inset panel × 1
3 = Wing × 4
4 = Muzzle × 2
5 = Eye × 2

Henrietta hen and chicks

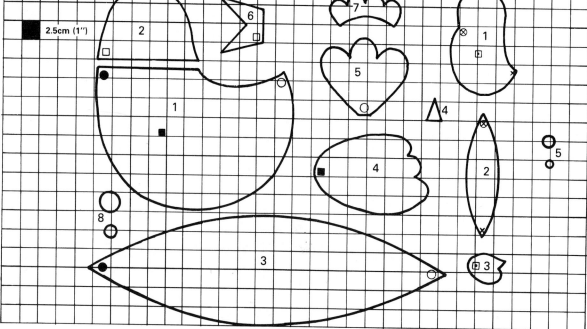

2.5cm (1″)

Henrietta Hen and chicks

To make up the design, follow the general instructions on pages 8–18. Be sure to check any special instructions and techniques used for this pattern. Any extra information is supplied as needed below.

The bodies of the 31cm (12⅛″) tall chicken and 14cm (5½″) tall chicks are formed from a simple profile shape.

Their plump outline is achieved with a wide body inset panel, tapering to a point at both ends.

On the hen the body, comb, tail and beak (all stuffed) and the wings (unstuffed) are all sewn on to the finished body with invisible stitches.

The chicks have felt beaks, and their wings are unstuffed too.

The legs are not meant to stand, as they are made from braided wool; draw the strands through the body fabric before braiding.

Fabric: gaily-colored oddments.

ROLY-POLY ANIMALS

The giant caterpillar shown here, and the owl and lion on page 75 are all made from cylinders which are about 35cm (13¾″) long. These can be made up into all sorts of appealing characters which are sturdy enough for small children to ride or sit on. They also make funny footstools and bolsters for grown-ups. They must be stuffed firmly to give good support, and are best made in tough, easy to clean fabrics, very important if they are to be used as footstools. Charlie, the giant caterpillar, can be any length you like, depending on how much fabric you have or how many riders he's likely to carry. As for Wisdom the owl and Leo the lion (page 75) they are just made from one section. You'll be able to dream up lots of animal characters yourself, using the basic pattern given here.

Roly-poly animals

To make up the design, follow the general instructions on pages 8–18. Be sure to check any special instructions and techniques used for this pattern. Any extra information is supplied as needed below.

Making these simple animals, all based on a rectangle and circle, should present no difficulties, even to the inexperienced. The same pattern makes them all; they only need their characteristic ears, wings and paws to complete them. Fabric requirements for the lining are the same as the cover.

First make a cylinder with the lining fabric (the same size for all the animals) and fill it with foam chips. Cut out the cover 1cm (¼″) larger all round. So that it can be taken off for cleaning, close the opening with a zip fastener. Sew the two circles to the body so that the seam is positioned on the belly for a figure lying down, and on the back for a standing one.

Charlie the Caterpillar

How many cylinders to put together for the giant caterpillar depends on the fabric available, or the number of children who would like to play on him.

Link the parts together with sewn-on tapes.

The feelers consist of very tightly-braided raffia; the nose is a circle, drawn up with a gathering thread and stuffed.

The cylindrical form can be used to make many more animals: for example a cat, dog or seal.

Fabric: 63 × 90cm (24⅞″ × 35½″) for each cylinder.

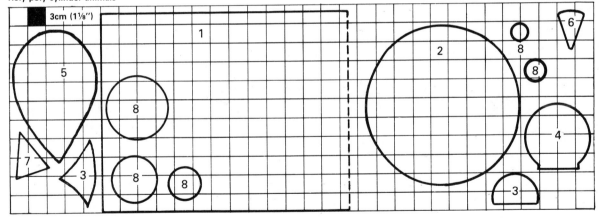

3cm (1⅛")

1

5

8

7

3

8

8

2

8

8

6

4

3

Roly-poly Animals
1 = Body × 2
2 = Head bottom piece or front/Back pieces
3 = Ear × 2
4 = Lion's paw × 2
5 = Wing × 2
6 = Nose × 1
7 = Beak × 1
8 = Eye × 2

Wisdom the Owl

For the owl, the cylinder stands upright. If you stuff him firmly enough he can be sat on, even by grown-ups. The wings should only be lightly stuffed.

Fabric: 35 × 140cm (13¾" × 55¼") for the body (without nap); 25 × 60cm (9¾" × 23¾") for ears and wings.

Leo the Lion

The lion, made from washable imitation leather, has a knotted-on woolly mane (see page 14) and a twisted woollen cord for a tail.

Fabric: 40 × 140cm (15¾" × 55¼"). (Imitation leather fabric).

Timmy the Tortoise; Biggles the Beetle

These brightly colored animals are very popular as 'realistic' floor cushions, though they are equally at home on chairs, beds and couches! They are about 36cm (14") across, and take very little time and effort to put together. Babies like them for a quick snooze on ground level, and if they are very firmly stuffed, they make nice footrests.

Tortoise
1 = Body back × 1
2 = Belly × 1
3 = Upper head piece × 2
4 = Lower head piece × 1
5 = Leg × 8
6 = Tail × 2
7 = Eye × 2

Beetle
1 = Body back × 2
2 = Belly × 1
3 = Head × 2
4 = Spot × 6
5 = Eye × 2

Timmy the tortoise;   Biggles the beetle

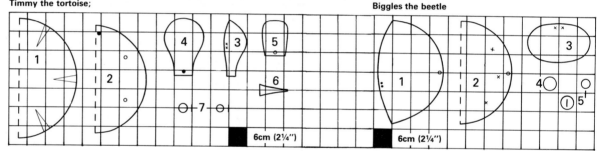

6cm (2¼")   6cm (2¼")

Timmy the Tortoise

To make up the design, follow the general instructions on pages 8–18. Be sure to check any special instructions and techniques used for this pattern. Any extra information is supplied as needed below.

On this delightful cushion the curve of the back is created by six darts, which should be sewn first.

Mark the circles on the pattern, transfer them to the fabric and embroider them in chain stitch.

Then sew the belly and back together, also the two upper head pieces, along the edge marked xx; join this to the lower head piece.

After stuffing sew the head, legs and tail to the belly.
Fabric: 40 × 75cm (15¾" × 29½") for the body; 20 × 90cm (7⅞" × 35½") for head, legs and tail.

Biggles the Beetle

To make up the design, follow the general instructions on pages 8–18. Be sure to check any special instructions and techniques used for this pattern. Any extra information is supplied as needed below.

The spots are embroidered in chain stitch, as described on page 13 under 'dolls' eyes'.

Here the rounded shape is produced by a curved centre seam (indicated by . .) on the back pieces.

Close this seam first, then sew the back to the belly. Position the finished head, firmly stuffed, on the front of the stuffed body.

The feet consist of woollen braids, the feelers of raffia braids.

So they can stand up to rough handling, draw the strands 20cm (7⅞") long for the feet, 40cm (15¾") long for the feelers, in any number divisible by three halfway through the fabric at the spots marked x and braid them.

To finish, bind the braid around; for the feelers knot and leave little tassels. For the nose sew on a 2cm (¾") ball button very firmly; if the beetle is meant for a very small child a woolly pompon is better, as it is not so likely to be bitten off.
Fabric: 45 × 65cm (18" × 25¾"); for the head an oddment, 45 × 15cm (18" × 6").

Four-legged animals

General instructions

The following patterns are more realistic. If you do not follow the grid patterns given, and create other animals of your own, careful attention must be paid to the relative proportions. Two methods are possible:

1. Draw the whole figure from a side view (profile).
2. Use the same principle but make the body pattern only, and draw the head separately as a front view.

Method 1: For an example of this type of pattern see below. Any profile view can be used, taken from a photograph or a drawing in a child's book and greatly simplified.

Drawing an outline immediately gives a pattern for all the body parts, and this outline can convey many different animals in different positions.

So that the animal stands on four legs, a centre panel is inserted.

This is cut from the lower part of the main body pattern, but ends at the broken line.

Both the main body pattern and the inset panel pattern are cut twice.

The legs can be drawn so that the animal stands, lies down or sits; the construction of the body with the inset panel still remains the same, but a slight alteration may be needed at the neck.

By comparing the patterns for the three small bears on page 84 you can see how to draw the same animal standing, lying or sitting.

Of course, many further variations are possible. If the animal is to stand do not make the legs too thin.

For large animals it is best to set soles into the bottoms of the legs, in order to give them more stability. Small animals do not need these.

The head should not come too far forward, or the animal will overbalance. To avoid any danger of this the head can be cut and sewn separately from the body, so that its position, and the correct balance, can be adjusted when it is attached.

However, when drawing patterns for your own creations, to get the best proportions first draw head and body all in one, and then divide pattern at the neck (e.g. pattern on page 78).

Heads shown in profile have a centre panel which is set in between the two side head pieces. This usually reaches from the neck front, past the tip of the nose or the forehead to the back of the head, or nape.

On fur fabric, or any fabric with a nap, the head should be made in two halves, with the pile running in opposite directions (see also page 11 under cutting).

Sometimes two head panels are necessary, drawn separately from the beginning.

The panel can also narrow at the eyes, and be widened by the meeting of the muzzle, forehead and upper head parts.

Sometimes a short panel reaching from the forehead to the back of the head is sufficient.

Method 2: The pattern for the body is drawn as described for method 1. The head is drawn separately and facing front.

A centre panel may also be inserted, but is only required for larger animals (e.g. the hippo on page 80).

Methods 1 and 2: Animals with either head shape can also have an additional inset panel down the back; this is recommended if a fat, stocky body is required.

All that remains is to draw the characteristic ears, and possibly a tail.

Making up

If darts are shown on the pattern sew these first. Then join the body inset panels together along the upper edge (the dividing line on the pattern), right sides together, leaving an opening in the middle for stuffing.

For small animals make this 10cm (4″), for larger ones about 20cm (8″) long. Then sew the finished panel in between the two main body pieces.

If soles are to be added, leave the lower edges of the legs open at first.

Sew the back seam, or where applicable insert the back panel.

Sew on the soles, if they are used.

Set the head inset panel between the two head pieces, paying attention to the direction of the fabric grain or pile.

Where head and body are separate, leave both open at the neck edges.

Turn the pieces out, stuff head and body and close the opening in the belly.

If the head is separate, attach it to the body opening.

Sew the ears together (generally these are not stuffed), pleat or gather the lower edge and sew to the head. Add the tail.

Additional instructions are given on pages 8–18.

Pedro the Spanish donkey

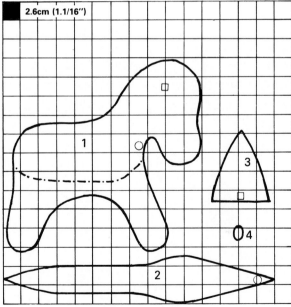

2.6cm (1.1/16″)

Pedro the Donkey
1 = Body × 2
    Body inset panel × 2
2 = Head inset panel × 1
3 = Ear × 4
4 = Eye × 2

Pedro the Spanish Donkey

What a proud little fellow Pedro is, with his brightly decorated blanket and smart little bridle. He looks as if he can hardly wait to trot out in style! Pedro is the first in a series of patterns which make up into four-legged animals. To stand securely, these animals need firm and expert stuffing.

Baby Puppies

Children who love puppies will be delighted to be given one of these adorable little creatures. Make the pattern up in a cuddly fabric, which can be plain or patterned as you prefer. The pups are not of any particular breed, so if you don't feel confident of your skills in producing more 'realistic' looking animals, then these would be ideal to make up.

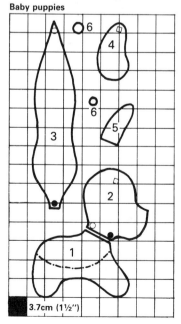

Baby puppies

3.7cm (1½")

78

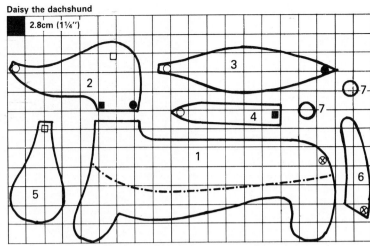

2.8cm (1¼")

3

2

7

7

4

1

5

6

Dachshund
1 = Body × 2
2 = Body inset panel × 2
3 = Upper head inset panel × 1
4 = Lower head inset panel × 1
5 = Ear × 2
6 = Tail × 1
7 = Eye × 2

Daisy the Dachshund

If one of your friends has a member of this delightful breed, they will be truly complimented to receive Daisy as a mascot gift. Children enjoy these funny little dogs too. Speciality breed dogs are fun to give to proud owners, but if you decide to draw up your own pattern, make sure the shape is very distinctive, like Daisy's.

Puppies (opposite)
1 = Body × 2
Body inset panel × 2
2 = Head × 2
3 = Head inset panel × 1
4 = Ear × 4
5 = Tail × 2
6 = Eye × 2

Pedro the Spanish Donkey

To make up the design, follow the general instructions on pages 8–18 and the instructions for four-legged animals above. Be sure to check any special instructions and techniques used for this pattern. Any extra information is supplied as needed below.

To make this 28cm (11″) tall donkey proceed as follows. The ears are stitched together first, and then sewn on.

The mane is made from separate bundles of raffia (see page 14), sewn on in close rows; the tail is a raffia tassel.

If the raffia is dampened before use it will stay in the desired position when dry. Fancy braid makes the bridle and edges the blanket.

Fabric: 30 × 110cm (11¾″ × 43½″) (without nap); scraps for the ear linings and blanket.

Baby Puppies

To make up the design, follow the general instructions on pages 8–18. Be sure to check any special instructions and techniques used for this pattern. Any extra information is supplied as needed below.

As already mentioned at the beginning, you must be careful when designing your own animals to alter the proportions when increasing the size.

For example the four puppies show that on little figures, a head which is over-size in proportion to the body looks very appealing.

On a larger dog, a head in the same proportion would look alarmingly big.

For general instructions on making up all the dogs see text on page 77, and for cutting the head inset panel see page 11.

All four puppies are 22cm (8⅝″) high, and made from the same pattern using oddments of fabric. For noses fix on buttons or pompons, 2cm (¾″) across.

Fabric: 45 × 50cm (18″ × 19¾″) for body and head, 45 × 13cm (18″ × 5″) for ears and tail (each puppy).

Otherwise, use remnants throughout, cutting the head and body panels in different fabrics.

Daisy the Dachshund

To make up the design, follow the general instructions on pages 8–18 and the instructions for four-legged animals on page 77. Be sure to check any special instructions and techniques used for this pattern. Any extra information is supplied as needed below.

The 50cm (19¾″) long dachshund has two separate inset panels on the head.

The small opening remaining at the tip of the muzzle after sewing should be drawn together with running stitches and covered with a 2cm (¾″) black fabric button or pompon.

Fabric: 45 × 100cm (18″ × 39½″).

Special breeds

For a child's toy it doesn't matter a bit what breed a dog belongs to, as outright mongrels can look most amusing and original. However for fans of a particular breed it is easy to draw the desired shape.

If you have already made several animals from the patterns given here you will be more likely to succeed in your own creation.

The main thing is to bring out the most striking features of the breed, for example short or long legs, blunt or pointed muzzle, the floppy ears of a dachshund or the high forehead of a poodle.

Dogs with long thin legs are best made in a sitting position.

For a poodle use a curly-pile fabric.

A dachshund's coat can be made equally well with a short- or long-pile fabric, showing fur in all lengths and textures.

Horace the Hippo

Who but the most stony-hearted could resist this fellow! Horace the hippo is 62cm (24½″) long, and strong enough for a child to sit on. Since Horace has such a flat face, he is an ideal subject on whom to experiment with different facial expressions. By exaggerating the curve of the mouth, up or downwards, and adding lines on the eyes and forehead, you can create all kinds of faces – sad and happy. Sketch out ideas on pieces cut out in paper from the head pattern, until you get the result that you like best. Then transfer onto the fabric, which should be a fairly smooth pile, otherwise the features disappear.

Horace the Hippo

To make up the design, follow the general instructions on pages 8–18 and the instructions for four-legged animals on page 77. Be sure to check any special instructions and techniques used for this pattern. Any extra information is supplied as needed below.

The patterns for the four-legged animals shown up to now have been made with the heads drawn in profile. Some have been cut in one with the body, others have been sewn on.

Here the body is shown in profile as far as the neck, and the head is separate and drawn full face.

Draw the pattern and sew the pieces together as described on page 77.

The head pieces include an inset panel that runs up to eye level.

The back, too, is widened by an inset panel shaped with darts, so that the body, as befits a hippopotamus, looks really massive.

Soles are placed in the bottoms of the legs.

To make the legs more sturdy, before stuffing the body insert a wooden dowel into each leg. This should be about 10cm (4″) long and wound around with scraps of fabric.

Take care to stuff very firmly both around and above these dowels.

The neck opening remaining on the body will be covered when sewing on the head; place the body neck to the centre of the back of the head.

Horace the hippo

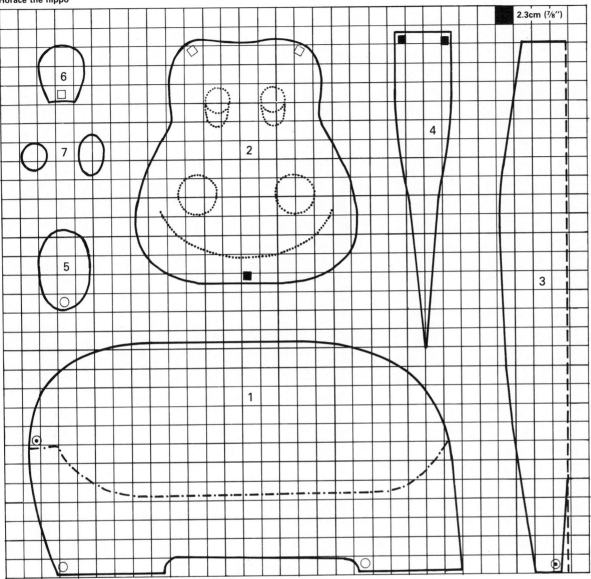

2.3cm (⅞'')

Horace the Hippo
1 = Body × 2
    Body inset panel × 2
2 = Head × 2
3 = Back inset panel × 1
4 = Head inset panel × 2
5 = Sole × 4
6 = Ear = 4
7 = Eye × 2

The head, ears and woolly braided tail should be sewn on very firmly with strong thread.

Fabric: 85 × 130cm (33¾'' × 51¼'') (without nap); an oddment for ear linings.

Polar Bear family

Children who love bears as toy pets, will be specially thrilled with this family group. In fact you can make the pattern up in dark brown fabric to make a common brown bear. For polar creatures, use white or very pale yellow fabric – try to get it as shaggy as possible to enhance the 'wild' look. Fabrics can change the appearance of these creatures dramatically – for example, the small bear (centre right) in the picture is the same pattern as the little brown bear in the collection on page 85!

Polar Bear family

To make up the design, follow the general instructions on pages 8–18 and the instructions for four-legged animals on page 77. Be sure to check any special instructions and techniques used for this pattern. Any extra information is supplied as needed below.

Draw the patterns and make up as described on page 77. For a more realistic appearance the muzzles can be drawn more pointed; however the head inset panel must then be lengthened correspondingly.

On the large bear the short muzzle has been purposely reduced, to lend this dangerous predatory animal a more authentic appearance.

On the cubs the muzzles are even more blunt.

The noses, consisting of two pieces without additions, should be sewn together with small overhand stitches.

Tails, ears, noses and eyes (unless closed) are the same for all three small bears.

Fabric: 85 × 150cm (33½″ × 59¼″) for the mother bear; 25 × 150cm (9¾″ × 59¼″) for each baby bear.

Zoo collection I

In this picture you are shown designs for animals which you can point out to your child on visits to the zoo. There's a crouching lion, a stately camel, a baby horse, a fierce alligator and a sweet baby seal. Many young children are interested in wildlife, and care about conservation.

Sealion
1 = Body × 2
2 = Belly Piece × 1
3 = Head inset panel × 1
4 = Rear fin × 2
5 = Front fin × 4
6 = Tail × 2
7 = Eye × 2

Alligator
1 = Body back piece × 2
2 = Belly piece × 1
3 = Leg × 8
4 = Mouth × 2
5 = Forehead × 2
6 = Teeth × 29
7 = Eye × 2

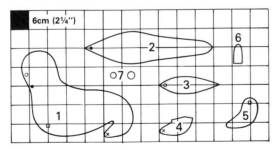

6cm (2¼")

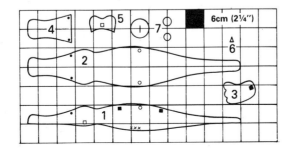

6cm (2¼")

Zoo collections

Standing animals

To make up the design, follow the general instructions on pages 8–18 and the instructions for four-legged animals on page 77. Be sure to check any special instructions and techniques used for this pattern. Any extra information is supplied as needed below.

Giraffe picture page 85: Height 50cm (19¾").

The horns and tail are made from rolled-up strips of fabric.

A 3cm (1⅛") long piece of fur fabric forms the tail tuft; the mane consists of a strip of fur fabric 25cm (9¾") long by 2cm (¾") wide, sewn in place; otherwise make a wool fringe (see page 14).

Mouth and nose are embroidered with curved lines and two small satin stitches.

Fabric: 55 × 80cm (21¾" × 31½"); an oddment for ear linings.

Hippo picture page 85: Length 45cm (18").

For the portly body a back inset panel is necessary.

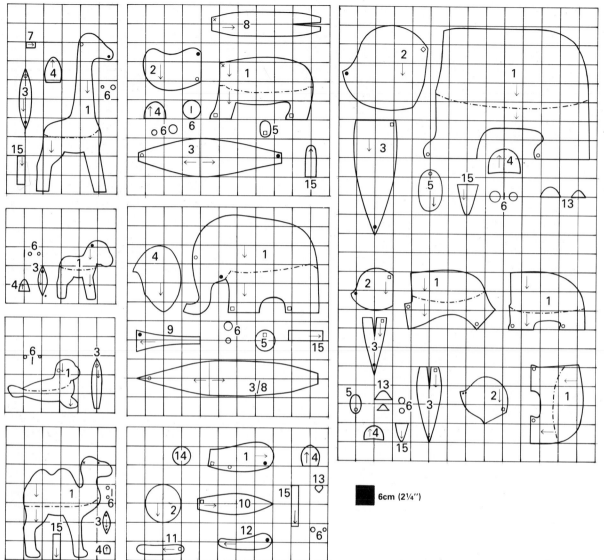

Polar bear, giraffe, pony, baby sealion, camel, hippo, elephant, lion

1 = Body × 2
      Body inset panel × 2
2 = Head × 2
3 = Head inset panel × 1
4 = Ear × 4
5 = Sole × 4
6 = Eye × 2
7 = Horn × 2
8 = Back inset panel × 1
9 = Trunk inset panel × 1
10 = Belly piece × 1
11 = Front leg × 4
12 = Back leg × 4
13 = Nose/nose piece × 1 each
14 = Muzzle × 2
15 = Tail – for polar bear and hippo × 2, for the others × 1

■ 6cm (2¼")

This lies between the tops of the body pieces. The eyes consist of three pieces, as described for the alligator on page 83. The mouth is embroidered on, beginning at one side of the head and running around to the other; embroider two circles for nostrils.

Fabric: 35 × 140cm (13¾" × 55¼"); a remnant for ear linings.

Elephant picture page 85: Height 34cm (13¼").

The shape has been made rather stocky, so that the animal is stable enough for grown-ups to use as a footstool, or for small children to sit on.

In the proportions given here, however, it is *not* intended as an animal which will take too much rough treatment.

As well as the body inset panel it has a trunk inset panel and yet another one which reaches from the forehead to the rear end. This may need to be made from

two pieces joined together (see page 11 under cutting).

The opening in the trunk should be drawn up with a gathering thread.

The mouth consists of a 12cm (4¾") long shoelace, and a wool tassel finishes the rolled tail.

The addition of a pretty blanket will add to his charm, and at the same time protect the back from wear and tear.

Fabric: 60 × 140cm (23¾" × 55¼"); an oddment for ear linings.

Brown bear picture page 85.

This is made with the same pattern as for the small standing polar bear pictured on page 82, but using a smoother fabric. For instructions see pages 77 and 82.

Camel picture page 83: Height 31cm (12⅛").
Make the body with a camel-colored woolly fabric.

Zoo collection II

This is the second in our collection of zoo animals. Here you will find a giraffe, a hippo, an elephant, a brown bear (made from the same pattern as one of the baby bears on page 82) and also a playful sealion. Does your child know how to identify the animals? Here's a good chance to learn.

Once the animal is stuffed sew on strips of shaggy fur fabric or fur, 13 × 5cm (5″ × 2″) on the head and neck, 11 × 6cm (4¼″ × 2¼″) on the chest; or knot on wool fringing (see page 14). Make up the ears and sew on.

For the nose embroider three satin stitches, for the mouth a curved line.

Fabric: 35 × 112cm (13¾″ × 44¼″); scraps of fur or fur fabric; an oddment for ear linings.

Pony picture page 83: Height 17cm (6¾″).

The mane consists of a strip of fur fabric, 12 × 13cm (4¾″ × 5″); the tail is a 7cm (2¾″) long piece of fabric, rolled up. Put the ears together and sew on.

Fabric: 22 × 75cm (8⅝″ × 29½″), plus fur fabric scraps and an oddment for ear linings.

Baby seal picture page 83: Length 23cm (9″).

This pattern is similar to that for four-legged animals. It is made up in the same way, as described on page 77, but instead of hind legs the seal has tail flippers.

As before, the body inset panel is copied from the main body pattern up to the broken line.

The head inset panel reaches from the front of the neck to the nape.

When inserting the body inset panel and closing the back seam leave the tail flipper sections open at first, then sew them together so that they make a pair.

The nose is embroidered with three satin stitches, the mouth is a curved line.

Fabric: 20 × 80cm (7⅞″ × 31½″).

Sealion picture page 85: Length 35cm (13¾″).

Here the body shape is constructed in a completely different way from that of the other zoo animals.

The belly piece, head inset panel and the two rear flippers are sewn in between the main body pieces, then the back seam is closed.

Cut an opening in the centre of the belly for turning and stuffing and close it with hand stitches.

For the whiskers draw nylon threads through the muzzle and knot them together where they emerge.

For the nose fasten on a 2cm (¾″) button. The mouth is an embroidered curved line.

Make up the front flippers, stuff lightly and sew by

85

hand to the sides of the body as shown in the photograph.

Finally attach the tail.

Fabric: 50 × 90cm (19¾″ × 35½″).

Lion picture page 84: length 26cm (10¼″).
This body is made as follows.

A belly panel is sewn between the two main body pieces, then the back seam is closed.

The legs are made separately and set onto the sides of the body after stuffing.

The neck opening on the body is fastened to the rear of the head, made from two circles, stitched and stuffed.

After sewing on the two round muzzle pieces, with the nose in between, embroider on two curves for the mouth.

Once the ears are in place sew small bundles of wool around the head, close together (see page 14).

Fix a wool tassel to the tail.

Fabric: 35 × 90cm (13¼″ × 35½″).

Alligator picture page 83: Length 72cm (28¼″).
When drawing up the pattern make quite sure that the sides of the back and belly pieces match exactly.

First sew the body back pieces together down the spine (marked xxx) then sew the completed back to the belly piece down the side seams, as far as the black dot on the head.

Set the red mouth inset panels into the head opening.

After stuffing, fix the forehead piece, stuffed but left open underneath, to the head.

The eyes each consist of three parts. Cut the largest pieces in fabric and gather them up around the edges, insert 2.5cm (1″) buttons and glue the white and black felt circles on top.

Set the feet onto the sides of the body.

Sew the 29 felt teeth on with small stitches so that when the mouth closes the upper ones fit into the gaps on the lower jaw.

Fabric: 45 × 90cm (18″ × 35½″); a scrap of red, without nap, for the mouth.

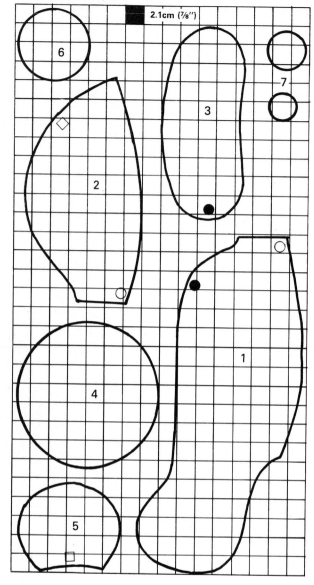

Bruno the giant teddy bear

2.1cm (⅞″)

Teddy Bear
1 = Body × 4
2 = Head × 4
3 = Arm × 4
4 = Muzzle × 1
5 = Ear × 4
6 = Nose × 1
7 = Eye × 2

Bruno the giant Teddy Bear

Here is a wonderful traditional teddy bear. The pattern is not so hard to draw as it might appear at first sight. The body is in the shape of a trouser pattern, on which the centre seam line, like that on the head, is made from a half circle so that it curves outwards slightly.

First join each pair of head pieces along this centre line, then sew together around the outside edge, leaving the neck open.

For the body, again first sew the pieces together in pairs down the centre seam, then lay them together and close the side and inner leg seams all in one.

Draw the round muzzle piece up to a diameter of 13.5cm (5¼″) with a gathering thread, stuff and sew to the front of the head.

The black nose is made in the same way, and should be gathered to a diameter of 6cm (2¼″). Make small pleats at the base of the ears and sew on, like all the other parts, with very small firm stitching. The pattern is on page 86, opposite.
Fabric: 50 × 140cm (19¾″ × 55¼″). Fleecy lining fabric is good.

Bruno the giant Teddy Bear

Every child needs a giant teddy bear of their own to hug closely and provide solid security. This Bruno is beautiful and solemn, and stands 60cm (23¾″) tall. He makes a lovely friend. You could make him from a discarded overcoat; if you have one made in a 'teddy bear' fabric that would be ideal. Another alternative is a fleecy coat lining. To make Bruno complete, put a loud 'growler' in his tummy – you can get one at a crafts store which has toy making accessories.

Bonzo the Boxer; Lazy Jumbo; Twee the cuddly Duckling

Lazy Jumbo! He's either just sitting up, or lying flat on his face, see opposite. He's quite irresistible, however, and a completely different design from the elephant in the zoo collection. Also flat on his tummy is Bonzo the boxer, a wonderful friend to all children. They are accompanied by

Twee, the cuddly duckling, made in the brightest sunshine yellow fabric we could find.

Bonzo the Boxer

To make up the design, follow the general instructions on pages 8–18. Be sure to check any special instructions and techniques used for this pattern. Any extra information is supplied as needed below.

To draw the pattern for this 50cm (19¾″) long boxer dog follow the instructions given for the elephant on page 85.

First sew the two body back pieces together down the spine and join the rear piece on to the outward curving edge, as far as the two black dots (. .).

Then sew body front to the back and rear pieces; also sew the front, rear and lower head pieces together.

Slightly draw up the centre of the face, and the inside halves of the ears, with a gathering thread.

After stuffing place the open neck of the body to the rear of the head and sew together.

The ears should be sewn on so that they stand up at first, then fall forward.

For this type of head the best kind of eyes are white fabric buttons with glued-on felt pupils.

For the nose fix on a 3cm (1⅛″) half ball button or a woolly pompon.

Fabric: 60 × 145 cm (23¾″ × 57¼″).

Twee the cuddly Duckling

To make up the design, follow the general instructions on pages 8–18. Be sure to check any special instructions and techniques used for this pattern. Any extra information is supplied as needed below.

The 48cm (19″) high duckling, soft and cuddly, uses the trouser pattern design first employed for Bruno the teddy bear (see page 87).

First sew the two front pieces together down the middle, and the two back pieces together down the middle.

Place together and sew the side and inner leg seams.

After stuffing the body place the feet, lightly stuffed, in the leg openings.

Sew the neck opening to the back of the head.

The wings are fastened on unstuffed; the tail is stuffed and sewn to the back.

Fix a bundle of 10cm (4″) lengths of wool to the top of the head (see page 14).

When sewing on the lightly stuffed beak pieces place the two sections close together.

The pattern is on page 91.

Fabric: 23 × 130cm (9″ × 51¼″) in yellow; a scrap of red 28 × 28cm (11″ × 11″).

Lazy Jumbo

To make up the design, follow the general instructions on pages 8–18. Be sure to check any special instructions and techniques used for this pattern. Any extra information is supplied as needed below.

This elephant is made so that it can both sit or lie down! It is not difficult to make provided the pattern pieces are drawn accurately, and put together in accordance with the guide marks.

First sew the darts. Sew the head inset panel and the large trunk inset panel in between the main head pieces and finish the trunk with the small circular piece.

Join the two body front pieces together down the belly, the body back pieces down the spine, and then set the hind piece on to the outward-curving edge of the body back, as far as the two black dots (. .).

Now join the front, rear and back pieces and finally insert the soles of the feet.

Before sewing together the stuffed head and body draw both neck openings up slightly with a gathering thread.

The ears should be set into the upper sides of the head.

Roll up the strip of tail fabric and sew the edge down by hand; finish the end with a tassel.

The mouth consists of a 20cm (7⅞″) long piece of 'shoelace' thread.

Fabric: 140 × 150cm (58¼″ × 59¼″); a scrap of beige or pink for the soles, 52 × 13cm (20½″ × 5″).

If you don't want to give quite such a large animal to a very small child, the elephant can be made up half size, by drawing the grid with only 3cm (1⅛″) squares.

Paddy the Penguin; Thumper the Rabbit

This jolly penguin and his loveable rabbit friend are seen here with a stuffed frog – he must have leaped over from page 70. Paddy the penguin is a smart, very upright sort of fellow, about 40cm (15¾") tall. Because he comes from a cold climate, we thought he would like his own little scarf to wear. Thumper the baby rabbit will steal the heart of every child – he should be made in the softest fabric you can get.

Paddy the Penguin

To make up the design, follow the general instructions on pages 8–18. Be sure to check any special instructions and techniques used for this pattern. Any extra information is supplied as needed below.

Cut both the back parts from black fabric and sew together down centre back.

Sew the white chest pieces together down centre front. Join this to the black side pieces and to the face, which has a seam down centre front.

The wings, turned out and lightly stuffed, are joined in while sewing back to front.

To make the penguin into a cover or wrapper, make the bottom piece overlap in the centre (follow the outside line on the pattern) and close with buttons or a zipper.

If the body is stuffed cut the bottom piece along the inside line and close the seam by hand after stuffing.

Before sewing together the beak pieces make a dart in the upper one. Stuff the feet lightly, the beak more firmly.

Then secure the feet to the front of the bottom piece, and the beak to the head so that it sticks forward.

A fringed scarf, 60cm (23¾") long by 6cm (2¼") wide, suits our charming black and white friend particularly well; make this in double (single U.S.) crochet from gaily colored oddments of wool (knot the fringe in the same way as hair, see page 14).

Fabric: 42 × 75cm (16½" × 29½") in black; scraps of white, yellow and red for chest, feet and beak, all without nap.

Thumper the Rabbit

To make up the design, follow the general instructions on pages 8–18. Be sure to check any special instructions and techniques used for this pattern. Any extra information is supplied as needed below.

As an Easter bunny to treasure throughout the year this 22cm (8⅝″) long rabbit can be made in any color.

For cutting out and making up see page 77, general instructions for four-legged animals. Instead of a sewn tail you can use a woolly pompon (see page 94 for how to make).

For the little nose use either a half ball button, 14mm (⅝″) diameter; or satin stitching.

Fabric: 21 × 100cm (8¼″ × 39½″), plus scraps for ear linings and tail.

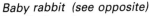

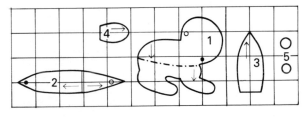

Baby rabbit (see opposite)
1 = Body × 2
    Body inset panel × 2
2 = Head inset panel × 1
3 = Ear × 4
4 = Tail × 2
5 = Eye × 2

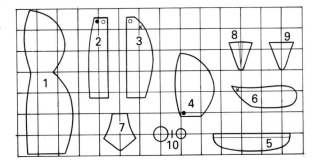

Penguin (see opposite)
1 = Back × 2
2 = Belly piece × 2
3 = Body side piece × 2
4 = Face × 2
5 = Bottom piece × 2
6 = Wing × 4
7 = Foot × 4
8 = Upper beak piece × 1
9 = Lower beak piece × 1
10 = Eye × 2

Elephant (see page 88)
1 = Back piece × 2
2 = Front piece × 2
3 = Rear piece × 1
4 = Head × 2
5 = Head inset panel × 1
6 = Trunk inset panel ×1

= Trunk piece × 1
8 = Sole × 4
9 = Ear × 4
10 = Tail × 1
11 = Eye × 2

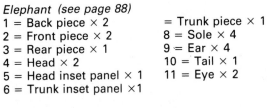

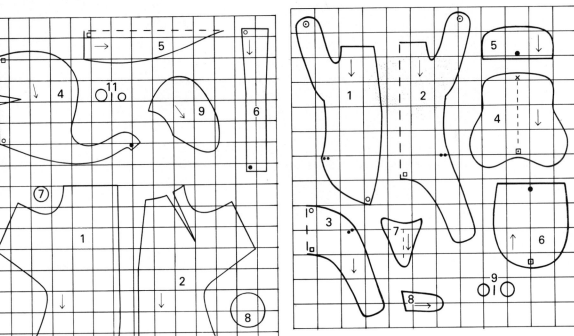

Boxer (see page 88)
1 = Back piece × 2
2 = Front piece × 1
3 = Rear piece × 1
4 = Front head piece × 1
5 = Back head piece × 1
6 = Lower head piece × 1
7 = Ear × 4
8 = Tail × 2
9 = Eye × 2

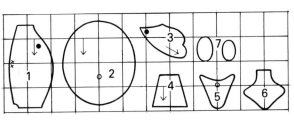

Duckling (see page 88)
1 = Body × 4
2 = Head × 2
3 = Wing × 4
4 = Tail × 2
5 = Muzzle × 4
6 = Foot × 4
7 = Eye × 2

Comic Dog;
Krazy Cat

Children simply adore these cartoon-like characters, and love to dress them up in their own clothes. Otherwise, you can make them some garments of their own from the easy patterns provided. These figures are really a combination of animal and doll, and are particularly liked by teenagers who might feel that they are too old for baby toys.

Comic Dog

To make up the design, follow the general instructions on pages 8–18. Be sure to check any special instructions and techniques used for this pattern. Any extra information is supplied as needed below.

To save expense one can make the body, arms and legs of this tall figure from fabric oddments, and only use 'fur' for the head, hands and feet.

Start by sewing the darts on the body, then join body front to body back.

For the feet cut two of the complete pattern piece, and two with the oval cut-out indicated; draw these up slightly with a gathering thread.

Stuff the hands and feet, arms and legs and sew together.

Make the elbow and knee joints by hand-stitching through the limb about half-way along.

Fasten limbs to body.

Sew the head inset panel, made in two pieces, in between head pieces.

Set the ears, unstuffed, onto the sides of the head so that they stick up and then fall down.

Sew the nose, made from two pieces, together with small overhand stitches, inserting a little cotton wool.

Sew the neck opening on the head to the body opening. Sew the trouser pieces together, hem the raw edges and insert elastic in the waist.

When cutting out the pullover from some cast-off knitwear, allow an extra 2cm (¾″) on the upper edge, and 1cm (⅜″) on all other edges.

Cut a slit in the back and turn the edges under.

Then sew the sleeves to the sides, and sew the side and shoulder seams as far as the marks shown on the pattern.

Sew a 2cm (¾″) shoulder seam; turn the neck opening inside by the same amount and catchstitch.

Fabric: For head, hands and feet, 35 × 145cm (13¾″ × 57¼″) fur fabric. For body, arms and legs, 50 × 130cm (19¾″ × 51¼″) any fabric. An oddment for ear linings. For the trousers, 70 × 70cm (27½″ × 27½″) fabric; for the pullover, something machine knitted to cut down.

Krazy Cat

To make up the design, follow the general instructions on pages 8–18. Be sure to check any special instructions and techniques used for this pattern. Any extra information is supplied as needed below.

Make up the body, arms and legs of the 100cm (39½″) tall cat exactly as for the dog.

If using towelling the head inset panel can be made in one piece, but with fur fabric it must have a seam in the centre.

Close the darts in the main, round head pieces and sew the inset panel to them so that the 'hairs' point downwards.

Cut a slit for turning and stuffing at the lower centre of this piece; this will be covered later by setting on the body.

After stuffing the larger paws to the legs and the smaller ones to the arms; sew securely.

Sew the ears to the edge of the upper head.

Pullover: knit the front and back as on the pattern adding a 1cm (⅜″) seam allowance. Start with the waist in knit 2, purl 2 rib and then continue in stocking stitch (knit 1 row, purl 1 row), leaving a slit open at back neck.

After closing the side and shoulder seams as far as the points marked on the pattern sew the arm edges under by 1cm (⅜″) and knit a 1.5cm (⅝″) band around the neck. Close the back opening with a button and loop.

Trousers: Begin knitting at the waistband edge and divide in the centre for the legs (see pattern).

After sewing the two pieces together thread elastic through the stitches at the waist.

Fabric: 60 × 140cm (23¾″ × 55¼″), plus 50 × 30cm (19¾″ × 11¾″) without nap for ears and paws.

For the clothes use up any gaily colored oddments of knitting wool.

Comic dog;

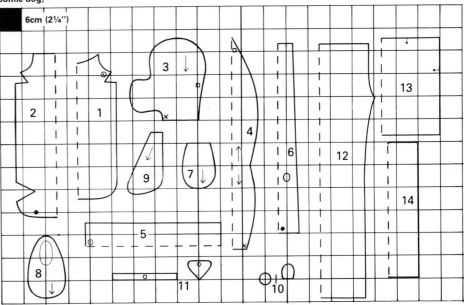

6cm (2¼″)

Krazy cat

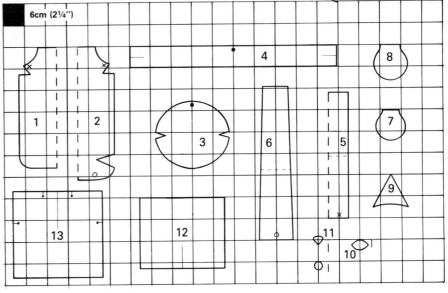

6cm (2¼″)

Comic Dog; Krazy Cat
1 = Body front × 1
2 = Body back × 1
3 = Head × 2
4 = Head inset panel × 1
5 = Arm × 2
6 = Leg × 4
7 = Hand (front paw) × 4
8 = Foot × 4
9 = Ear × 4
10 = Eye × 2
11 = Nose/nose piece × 1
12 = Trousers × 2
13 = Pullover × 2
14 = Sleeve × 2

93

How to make pompons

You can make pompons from odd scraps of yarn that you have no other use for. From pompons you can make all sorts of delightful toys – those shown in the pictures are a few examples. In fact the possibilities are endless, and you'll be able to make up all sorts of realistic and imaginary figures yourself.

Making the pompon

Cut two disks of equal size from a piece of card. To make a hole in the middle, lay the disks on top of each other, and cut through once (see photo page 95). Then cut out the inner circle. Wind the yarn from one side of the slit to the other, and then back again.

Measurements: To calculate the size of the disk required, first measure 1cm ($\frac{3}{8}$") out from the centre. This is the radius of the centre hole. Then take half the diameter of the required pompon. This equals the radius of the disk.

Example: For a pompon measuring 5cm (2") across, calculate as follows. Half the diameter = 2.5cm (1") = the radius of the disk. Set a pair of compasses to this radius, and draw a circle on a piece of doubled card.

Then adjust the compasses to 1cm ($\frac{3}{8}$") = radius of the centre hole, and draw the inner circle. Using sharp scissors, cut around the outer circle first. Then cut a slit as far as the edge of the inner circle. Now the inner circle can be cut out easily.

Wind the yarn around evenly until the centre hole is filled up. This will produce a good, solid pompon. Use less yarn for a looser pompon.

When the winding is completed, cut through the threads around the edges of the disk, and pull them apart slightly. Tie a short length of yarn firmly around the loops between the disks, and secure with a knot. Finally pull the disks away. Trim off any surplus pieces of yarn.

If felt features are to be glued onto the pompon, it will have to be made up solidly in order to hold the glue.

Small, dense pompons less than 2cm ($\frac{3}{4}$") across are difficult to make, so it is better to buy them from craft stores, or use something else e.g. a ball button for noses.

To make oval pompons, simply trim a round one to the desired shape.

To make figures stand upright, cut them flat underneath (for example the ladybird, duck, rabbit and mouse on page 95); this is not necessary on birds, because they will have legs.

Pompons intended to be sewn onto another part of the body can also be trimmed flat on the underside before sewing them on.

When several pompons are used together, for example to make a body, trim them after joining so that the divisions between them can no longer be seen (for example the body of the dog on page 101).

To allow for trimming make the disks about 1.5cm ($\frac{5}{8}$") larger than the finished diameter required.

For multi-colored pompons either twist different yarn oddments together and roll into a ball (this gives a streaky look, as on the hedgehog, page 98, or the puppy, page 97; or wind several different colored layers onto the disk (fish, page 95).

If you want two separate layers of color wind the disk half with one color and half with the second.

There are many more possible variations which you will think of for yourself.

Figures made from several pompons put together should be tightly bound with fine string, then threaded together and knotted firmly. If you need several pompons of the same size it is a good idea to divide the available yarn up equally first.

To sew on stuffed felt parts, thread a long darning needle with double thread. Stick it first through the felt where it will join the pompon, leaving a long end. Then stick the needle right through the pompon (if possible through the centre), put plenty of glue on the felt part, pull the threads tight and knot them together.

The set-on part will then be drawn firmly into the pompon.

Instructions for all pompon figures

Beaks, muzzles, mouths, ears, fins and feet should be glued firmly to the inside of the pompon (part the yarn to get the glue spread on). Pipe-cleaner legs, especially, will need plenty of glue; also, stand the figures upside down while it dries.

Facial features can be either glued on, or sewn by passing a needle right through the pompon several times. Make up the parts as shown in the photographs, put them together and secure. The measurements given for pompons and facial features are always *diameters*.

Pompon pets

Parrot
Yarn: 90g ($3\frac{1}{2}$oz) in two or more colors.
Size: body 10cm (4"), trimmed to make an oval; head 7cm ($2\frac{3}{4}$"). Lay the wing pieces together, smallest on top and matching up small 'Os'. Oversew round the edge as shown, padding with a little cotton wool. Sew the two tail pieces together round the straight edges, leaving the shaped bottom part open. Insert strands of yarn, 18–20cm (7–8") long, in this part and glue together. Sew the beak pieces together on the curved sides and stuff firmly.
Legs: see diagram, page 98. After glueing them into place wind them round with yarn at the top.

Monkey
Yarn: 60g ($2\frac{1}{2}$oz).
Size: body 8cm ($3\frac{1}{8}$"), trimmed to an oval; head 6.5cm ($2\frac{1}{2}$"). The muzzle is 4.5cm ($1\frac{3}{4}$") pompon, cut flat on one side and secured to the head with the round side uppermost. The mouth is a piece of yarn, laid on the muzzle and sewn in place. For arms and legs take 2 × 18 pieces of yarn, 65cm (25") long and thread through the body. Glue firmly in the centre. Work each limb into a braid, knot the ends and trim to form a tassel.

Birds
Yarn: 20g ($\frac{3}{4}$oz) in mixed bright colors.
Size: body 5.5cm ($2\frac{1}{8}$"); head 4.5cm ($1\frac{3}{4}$"). For legs see page 98.

Pompon pets

Here's a delightful bunch of pets to create from cuddly woollen pompons – and they're so easy to make too. Pompons can be wound from any leftover scraps of wool – even if it has been unravelled from a piece of knitted fabric! Here you can see a parrot, a monkey, several birds, a chick, a mouse, a duck, a ladybird, a frog and a rabbit. Patterns are on pages 94 and 96.

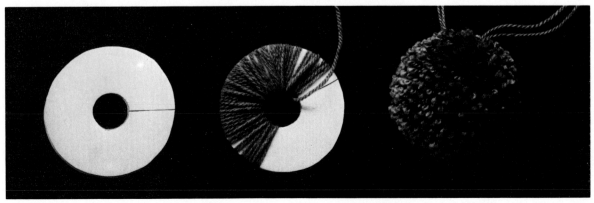

Chick
Yarn: 25g (1oz) in yellow.
Size: body 6cm (2⅜″); head 5cm (2″). For legs see page 98.

Fish
Yarn: 15g (½oz) in assorted colors.
Size: body 6cm (2⅜″). Wind the cardboard disks with several layers of different colored yarn. The fins and tail are loops of yarn glued in place.

Mouse
Yarn: 15g (½oz).
Size: body 4.5cm (1¾″); head 3.2cm (1¼″). For the tail cut 12cm (4¾″) long pieces of yarn and twist together. The nose is a 5mm (3/16″) ball, sewn on.

Duck
Yarn: 20g (¾oz) in mixed bright colors.
Size: body 8cm (3⅛″) cut to an oval; head 4.5cm (1¾″).

Ladybird
Yarn: 20g (¾oz).
Size: body 6cm (2⅜″); head 3cm (1⅛″). Trim the body flat where the head is to be attached. Bind the body with black yarn to mark the wings. Thread six strands of black yarn through from the back of the head to the front to make 4cm (1½″) long feelers finished with a tassel.

Frog
Yarn: 20g (¾oz).
Size: body 5.5cm (2⅛″); head 4cm (1½″); eyeballs 12mm (½″). Sew the mouth parts together along the concave edges and stick into the head.

Rabbit
Yarn: 45g (1½oz).
Size: body 8cm (3⅛″), trimmed to an oval; head 6cm (2⅜″). Paws and tail 2cm (¾″); nose ball 6mm (¼″).

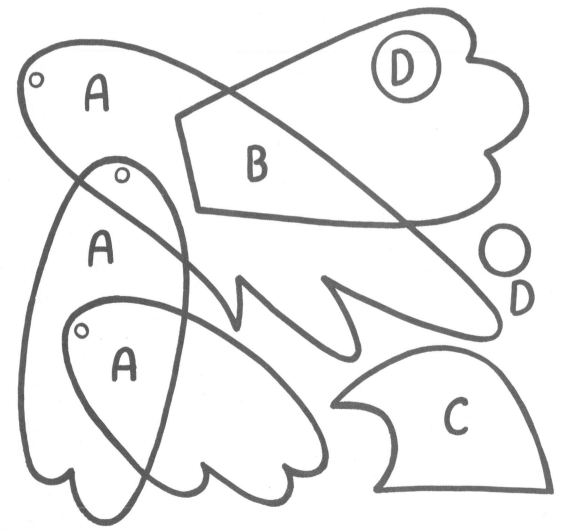

Pattern for the parrot
(actual size)
A = wings; B = tail;
C = beak; D = eyes.
Cut two of each piece

Slim Jim; Coo the Caterpillar; Dotty Poodle; Miss Mouse

Another delightful collection of woolly characters is shown here – a boy doll, a green caterpillar, a bright little poodle, and a tiny, inquisitive mouse. Figures like these have tremendous charm and bags of personality, yet the basic skill – making the pompons – is literally child's play. In fact, your child can be making up the pompons while you get on with putting all the parts together. Children like to feel they have a hand in creating things with you.

Slim Jim

To make a figure 47cm (18½″) high you will need 400g (14oz) of yarn oddments, plus 30g (1oz) for the hair. Also felt scraps.

Make the following pompons: body 2 × 8cm (3⅛″), arms and legs 14 × 4.5cm (1¾″), hand 2 × 3.5cm (1⅜″), feet 2 × 5.5cm (2⅛″). Head: make this from a 10cm (4″) polystyrene or cotton wool ball. This is covered with a piece cut from a pair of tights or a thin sock, drawing the folds around to the back.

Pierce through the centre of the head from top to bottom with a thick knitting needle, thread the binding string of the top pompon through this hole and secure. **Nose:** use half a 10mm (⅜″) ball button; **Mouth:** use a 3cm (1⅛″) length of yarn, stuck on (or embroidered).

Coo the Caterpillar

Caterpillar (33cm (12⅞″) long):
Yarn: 100g (3½oz) either one color or mixed. Make 4 6.5cm (2½″) body pompons and a 9cm (3½″) head. Eyes are 3/2cm (1⅛″/¾″); nose 2cm (¾″); topknot 6cm (2⅜″) long.

Miss Mouse

Pattern on page 100.
Yarn: 30g (1oz) body pompon is 6cm (2⅜″); eyes 12/10mm (½″/⅜″); nose ball 10mm (⅜″). Fold the ears as shown and sew to the head after stuffing it firmly. The tail is a 15cm (6″) braid of wool finished with a tassel. Glue the feet to the belly.

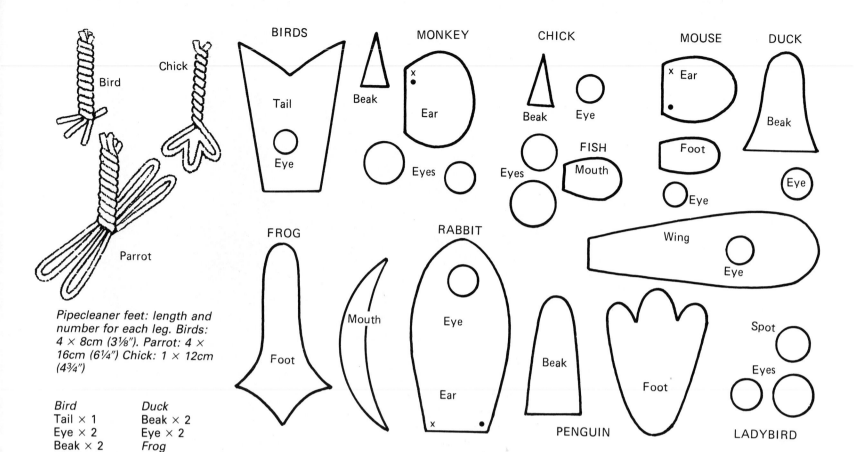

BIRDS
Tail
Eye

Beak

MONKEY
x
Ear

Eyes

CHICK
Beak

Eye

Eyes

FISH
Mouth

MOUSE
x Ear

Foot

Eye

DUCK
Beak

Eye

FROG
Mouth

Foot

RABBIT
Eye

Ear

x

PENGUIN
Beak

Foot

Wing
Eye

Spot

Eyes

LADYBIRD

Pipecleaner feet: length and number for each leg. Birds: 4 × 8cm (3⅛"). Parrot: 4 × 16cm (6¼") Chick: 1 × 12cm (4¾")

Bird	Duck
Tail × 1	Beak × 2
Eye × 2	Eye × 2
Beak × 2	*Frog*
Small monkey	Foot × 2
Ear × 2	Mouth × 2
Large eye × 2	*Hare*
Small eye × 2	Ear × 2
Chicks	Eye × 2
Beak × 2	*Penguin*
Eye × 2	Wing × 2
Fish	Eye × 2
Mouth × 2	Beak × 2
Large eye × 2	Foot × 2
Small eye × 2	*Beetle*
Mouse	Spot × 4
Ear × 2	Large eye × 2
Foot × 2	Small eye × 2
Eye × 2	

Dotty Poodle

Yarn: 85g (3oz) light beige and light brown mixed. Make 4 × 8cm (3⅛") pompons and form into one as described on page 94. Sew the 10cm (4") head pompon onto one end of the body. Then add a 7cm (2¾") muzzle pompon, with 22mm (⅞") nose. Make 4 × 3.5cm (1⅜") pompons for feet and a 5cm (2") one, cut down as shown, for the tail. The ears are loops of yarn wound round four fingers.
Eyes: 20mm (¾") white fabric buttons with 12mm (½") felt pupils.

Harriet Hedgehog and Family

The pattern for the head is on page 100; for instructions on how to sew the parts together see page 94.
Yarn: for the large hedgehog, 30g (1oz); for each little one 15g (½oz).

Use three strands of brown and one of beige, twisted together.

Make the head in yellow felt and stuff.

The pompons should be loosely made, 10cm (4") for the mother and 6.5cm (2½") for the babies.

Push the tip of the nose in slightly and sew on a 15 or 12mm (⅝"/½") black ball. Glue on the eyes, 15/12mm (⅝"/½") for the mother, 12/10mm (½"/⅜") for the babies.

Harriet Hedgehog and family

What do we see creeping quietly along? Perhaps this lovely little hedgehog family are out for an evening walk. These demure little animals are made from pompons wound in mixed colors. The patterns are on page 100.

98

Wisdom the Owl;
Sammy
the Squirrel

Two more wildlife creatures made from pompons are shown here perched watchfully along the tree branch. Wisdom the owl and Sammy the squirrel make fun gifts for friends of all ages – from nine to ninety. A life-size pattern for Sammy is shown below, while the pattern for Wisdom is on page 100.

Actual size pattern for squirrel.
A = tail; B = ear; C = legs

Wisdom the Owl

The pattern for the felt pieces is on page 100.
Yarn: 50g (1¾oz) of grey or mixed color yarn to make a 13cm (5″) pompon.

Fasten a small tuft of yarn between the grey felt ears.

Sew the yellow felt beak together along the curved edges and stuff firmly; sew on (see page 94).

Glue the yellow feet on underneath. Stuff the brown wings and fix them to the sides.

The eyes are 4cm (1½″) disks of green felt, with 3cm (1⅛″) pupils.

Sammy the Squirrel

The pattern for the felt parts is on page 100; for instructions on how to sew them together see page 94.
Yarn: 50g (1¾oz) of brown yarn to make an 8cm (3⅛″) body pompon, cut into an oval, and a 6cm (2⅜″) head; sew them together.

Sew together the arms, legs and tail pieces, stuff and sew on.

Fold the ears in the centre and glue to the head.

Sew rows of small bundles of 15cm (5½″) lengths of yarn (see page 14) close together on the upper side of the tail. Tease them out to look fluffy. Glue on 12/10mm (½″/⅜″) eyes.

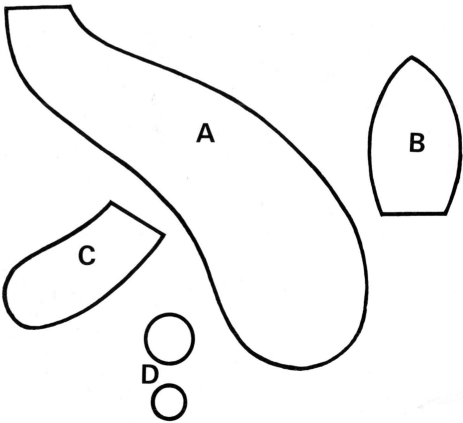

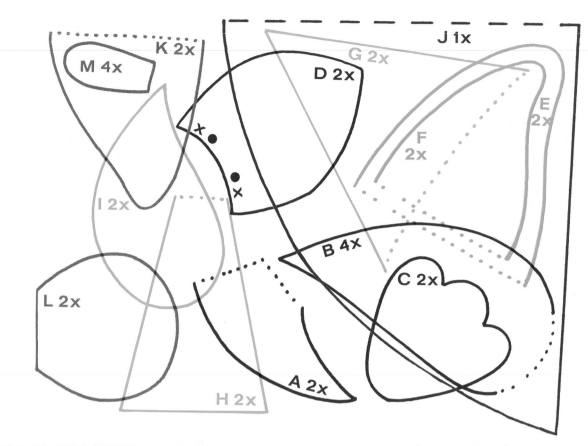

= Dwarf below
= Mouse page 97
= Owl page 99
= Hedgehog page 98
= Raven below
• • • • • = Leave open initially

A = Owl's beak
B = Owl's wing
C = Owl's foot
D = Owl's ear
E = Mother hedgehog's head
F = Baby hedgehog's head
G = Raven's beak
H = Raven's tail
I = Raven's wing
J = Dwarf's cap
K = Mouse's head
L = Mouse's ear
M = Mouse's foot

Tom Troll; Dib Dwarf; Caw the Raven

These jolly mascots are made in the twinkling of an eye. If you have some cotton wool or polystyrene balls, some odd scraps of felt and a dab of glue, then you're all set to go ahead. Use your own imagination to invent lots of other characters from the same basic pattern. The patterns for the mascots pictured here are shown above.

Tom Troll; Dib Dwarf; Caw the Raven

Many of the pompon figures already described can be made like these mascots, with ball bodies, which take up less yarn. Conversely, the mascots can also be made with pompons.

Start by smearing a 9cm (3½") diameter ball lightly with glue (the cement sold for model making is best for use with polystyrene). When it is tacky, wind yarn around to cover. This should always cross at the same point top and bottom, and cover the ball evenly. The eyes are then glued on, and a bead nose sewn on. To make arms and legs pass lengths of wool through the wool covering, braid together and knot the ends.

Tom Troll

His topknot is a loose pompon, 10cm (4″) across. Eyes are 20/15mm (¾″/⅝″), nose bead 2cm (¾″). The arms are made with six strands of yarn 28cm (11″) long, the legs with six strands 33cm (13″) long.

Dib Dwarf

Sew on a knitted band about halfway down the ball (alternatively, cut a piece from a child's sweater or sock). For his beard unravel some yarn from an old garment and sew on in loops (see page 14). The nose, a 12mm (½″) bead, goes on directly above the beard, also the 12/10mm (½″/⅜″) eyes. Place cap with seam at centre back.

Caw the Raven

Sew the beak together along the straight sides, stuff and sew to centre front of a yarn-covered ball. Make the tail in the same way and sew it on so it enables the figure to sit. Sew the wings to the sides and place a tuft of 6cm (2⅜″) strands of yarn on top. Use 9 yarn strands for the legs, 28cm (11″) long, and braid. Eyes are 25/20mm (1″/ ¾″).

Kim Clown; Dizzy Dog; Pip Penguin

Kim Clown: Any little girl or boy would love this small, soft clown. He takes about 50g (2oz) of yarn altogether. Pattern is on page 110.

Begin the legs separately ('a'): work 3 rows garter stitch, then change to stocking stitch. At 'b' put all the stitches on the needle and continue to work in stocking stitch. At 'c' knit every 2nd and 3rd stitch together for one row. Work 2 rows on the previously-reduced number of stitches, then increase 1 stitch after every 2nd stitch and continue straight. The color change for the cap occurs at 'd', and begins with 6 garter stitch rows. At 'e' knit together every 5th and 6th stitch and after the return row draw the stitches together with a thread.

Arms: knit straight pieces, beginning with 3 garter stitch rows, then change to stocking stitch.

Close seams, leaving openings in the head and back.

Hands: take the stitches on the garter stitch ends of the arms on to 4 needles and knit in pink. After 2.5cm (1″) knit 2 together all round, work one round, then draw the remaining stitches together.

Shoes: work in garter stitch as pattern, fold and sew together. Stuff all parts (the head can be 8cm (3″) polystyrene or cotton-wool ball) and sew together. Stick on 10mm (⅜″) eyes, a 6mm (¼″) nose in felt and embroider the mouth. Knot hair round the edges of the cap (see page 14). Pull the neck in with a gathering thread. Make a 5cm (2″) pompon for the cap and 2.5cm (1″) pompons for the body and sew on.

Dizzy Dog: This adorable little dog takes about two afternoons to make. He can be made from about 120g (4½oz) of 4-ply yarn, but it does not have to be all the same color – different oddments can be used for the knitted body and the knotted shaggy pelt. The pattern is on page 110.

Work in stocking stitch. Close the underneath seam, leaving a 5cm (2″) gap for filling; also close the front and

Kim Clown;
Dizzy Dog;
Pip Penguin

This happy trio of woolly toys are easy to make, and provide hours of fun. The clown and dog are knitted, while Pip the penguin is made from a pompon pattern.

back seams. Draw these last up slightly with a gathering thread. Also leave an opening at the base of the head. Put the centre panel on the front of the head, corners slightly rounded off, and gather the rear edge of the head. For ears, tail and legs make up the knitting reverse side out. After stuffing set the head on the body so that half of it sticks forward. Use gathering threads to give the animal shape, by drawing in the belly and centre of the head slightly from top to bottom. Then set strands of yarn on the lower half of the head so that they form a shaggy muzzle.

The front legs should be sewn on to stand, the back ones to sit. Sew on ears, unstuffed. For the shaggy pelt use 5cm (2″) lengths of yarn, double or even treble if the wool is thin, closely knotted onto the back (see page 14). Cut ends short to finish. For the topknot cut 7cm (2¾″) lengths of yarn; do not trim. The nose is a 25mm (1″) black pompon, the eyes 20/12mm (¾″/½″) felt disks.
Pip Penguin: Yarn, 20g (¾oz) each of black and white. Body 8cm (3⅛″) trimmed to an oval; head 6cm (2⅜″). Wind the cardboard disks' halfway round with black and half with white yarn. See general instructions on page 94.

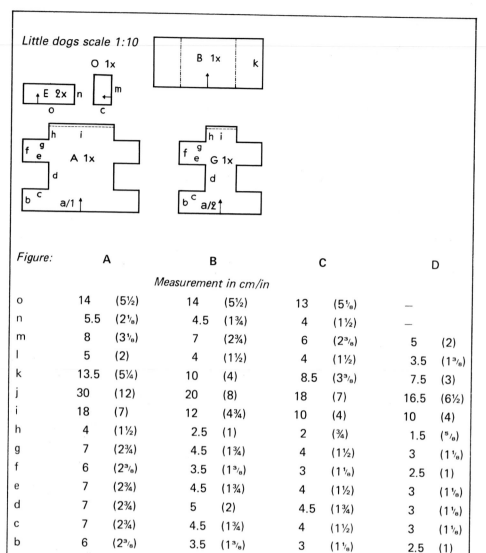

Little dogs scale 1:10

Figure:	A		B		C		D	
			Measurement in cm/in					
o	14	(5½)	14	(5½)	13	(5⅛)	—	
n	5.5	(2⅛)	4.5	(1¾)	4	(1½)	—	
m	8	(3⅛)	7	(2¾)	6	(2³⁄₈)	5	(2)
l	5	(2)	4	(1½)	4	(1½)	3.5	(1³⁄₈)
k	13.5	(5¼)	10	(4)	8.5	(3³⁄₈)	7.5	(3)
j	30	(12)	20	(8)	18	(7)	16.5	(6½)
i	18	(7)	12	(4¾)	10	(4)	10	(4)
h	4	(1½)	2.5	(1)	2	(¾)	1.5	(⁵⁄₈)
g	7	(2¾)	4.5	(1¾)	4	(1½)	3	(1⅛)
f	6	(2³⁄₈)	3.5	(1³⁄₈)	3	(1⅛)	2.5	(1)
e	7	(2¾)	4.5	(1¾)	4	(1½)	3	(1⅛)
d	7	(2¾)	5	(2)	4.5	(1¾)	3	(1⅛)
c	7	(2¾)	4.5	(1¾)	4	(1½)	3	(1⅛)
b	6	(2³⁄₈)	3.5	(1³⁄₈)	3	(1⅛)	2.5	(1)
a/2	22.5	(8¾)	16	(6¼)	14.5	(5¾)	11.5	(4½)
a/1	32	(12½)	21	(8¼)	18	(7)	16	(6¼)

Draw a pattern for the required size of dog, working from bottom to top, so that you reproduce the measurements given against the small letters, starting with a/1.

Fido; Flounce; Florrie; Fifi

Just a few moments of your time is all it takes to knit up one of these adorable little puppies. Woolly creatures such as these get hugged and squeezed with ecstasy, and they are loved by very small babies as well as toddlers. Stuff them with a washable filling so you can wash them often. A chart of measurements for each dog is provided opposite – the pattern is basically the same, with a little variation for each pup.

Fido; Flounce; Florrie; Fifi

If you have little time and lots of yarn remnants, twist together several strands in the colors of your choice and use medium-sized needles. In this way the largest dog in the group can be knitted in about 2½ hours. They can either sit up or stretch out, and so make good mascots to put in the back window of a car.

All four shown here are made from the same pattern (see opposite). For materials and measurements see Tables 1 and 2, on the opposite page. The stitch shown is garter stitch (every row knit).

Begin with the back of the body (A) at a/1. At 'c' cast off an equal number of stitches on each side for the hind legs. At 'e' cast on the stitches again and work the front legs as for the back legs. Fasten off all stitches at 'i' (neck). Work the underside (G) as for the back; it is exactly the same but narrower. Sew back and underside together. The head (B) should be sewn together so that the seam runs down the centre back; leave an opening for stuffing. Close the top and bottom head seams.

If you are giving the dog a white muzzle, run a gathering thread around the head starting under the muzzle, and draw this up to give the head shape – this shows most clearly in dog B.

The ears should not be stuffed. When sewing together the body and underside pieces leave a small opening at the back in which to insert the tail. The neck opening ('i') should be drawn up with a thread before fastening to the back of the head. Put the pompon muzzle on the face, then position the nose on the muzzle; or have a nose only, set in the centre. A red felt tongue can also be added.

With only a little more work you can make a shaggy dog (D). After making up as for the other dogs, lay 8.5cm (3⅜″) lengths of yarn over the back and head, close together, glue on lightly and secure with back stitches down the centre. Then make up bundles of yarn in the following lengths: under-muzzle 8cm (3⅛″), tail 6cm (2⅜″), topknot 7cm (2¾″), ears 15cm (6″), and sew in place.

Six woolly dolls

These darling little toys are all 16cm (6¼″) tall, and can be knitted up very fast. With a dash of ingenuity you can make all sorts of personalities by adding a mop of hair or a fuzzy beard, for example. Also, use accessories such as hats, scarves, bow ties made from scraps of ribbon, and pompon trims.

Six woolly dolls

(Pattern see page 110)

These little knitted figures, only 16cm (6¼″) high, can equally well be mascots or toys. Each one takes about 20-25g (¾-1oz) of 4-ply yarn in assorted bright colors. Begin with the legs at 'a' by casting on 20 stitches for each leg. Work in stocking stitch for 4.5cm (1¾″). Then at 'b' join the two sets of stitches onto one needle and continue working, in the different stitches shown, or according to your choice.

At 'c' change the yarn to pink (white or brown) for the face. Proceeding in stocking stitch work two rows. Next row: knit 1, (knit 2 together, knit 1) to end of row: 27 stitches. Work three rows straight. Next row: knit 2, (pick up loop lying between needles and knit into back of it) to last stitch, knit 1. Work straight to 'd'.

At this point change color and stitch for hair or cap if required. For a cap just work straight and draw the last row of stitches up with a thread.

For shaped heads decrease as follows on the knit rows: knit 4, (knit 2 together, knit 4) to end: 34 stitches. 2nd row: purl. 3rd row: knit 1, (knit 2 together, knit 1) to end: 23 stitches. 4th row: purl. 5th row: knit 1, (knit 2 together) to end. 6th row: purl. Draw up the remaining stitches with the end of the yarn. The seam runs down centre back; leave an opening for stuffing.

The arms are knitted separately and sewn to the body sides. To finish, draw up the neck slightly with a thread; you can also do the same to the arms to indicate wrists.

Hair can be made with embroidered loops (black doll, dwarf, clown) or knotted (blonde doll) – see page 14. The white hands of the clown are a little longer than those of the other dolls. To the red skirt add two knitted shoulder straps, 1cm (⅜″) wide and 10cm (4″) long, sewn on crossing at the back. The 'winter doll' has a scarf 30cm (12″) long and 2cm (¾″) wide.

Bounce the Clown and Baby Calf

Bounce the clown and his friend the baby calf are talking over the farm fence. The baby calf is 35cm (13¾") long, and can be made from a cut-up old pullover that you no longer wear. Bounce is 43cm (16⅞") tall and is easily knitted up from odd scraps of wool. Since he has to perform in the circus, choose the brightest colors that you can find, and make him a hat from a cut-off pullover sleeve. He'll need some smart pompons to trim his outfit.

Bounce the Clown

(Pattern see page 110)
This gaily-striped figure stands 43cm (17") high and takes 150g (5½oz) of yarn. First work the legs separately, in stocking stitch stripes, and when they are 10.5cm (4⅛") long join the stitches together on one needle and work. The head is made separately. After stuffing all the parts, put the arms on across the shoulder seams. For the collar knit a strip 50cm (20") long and 4.5cm (1¾") wide in knit 1 purl 1 rib, draw up with a thread and sew round the neck.

For the nose cover a 22mm (⅞") ball button with fabric of felt. The eyes are 25/20mm (1/¾") felt disks, the mouth two 3cm (1⅛") long stitches. Knot the hair using 11.5cm (4½") lengths of yarn (see page 14). The cap is made from part of a pullover sleeve, 30cm (12") long and gathered together at the wrist end. Turn the other end under 5cm (2") and back 3cm (1⅛"). Make three 4.5cm (1¾") pompons for the cap and body.
Shoes: garter stitch from 'a' to 'b', then cast off to reduce width by 2cm (¾") on each side and continue to 'c'. Next row: knit 2 together. Next row: purl. Draw together the remaining stitches. Fold in half and close back and front seams.

Baby Calf

(Pattern see page 110).
Sew the back and belly together. The head part should be sewn together so that the seam runs down the centre back, leaving an opening for stuffing.

Close the top and bottom head seams. Stuff and fasten the ears to the sides of the head.

For the muzzle first close the side seams. Open each seam out and pull into a point at the bottom; sew horizontally across this to give the muzzle shape.

Stuff and sew onto the head. On the head fix 12 bundles of yellow yarn each with about 12 strands, 10cm (4") long (see page 14).

Finish the tail with a tassel. The nostrils are two pink circles embroidered on the muzzle; the felt eye disks are 25/22mm (1"/⅞").

Snug and Cozy

These appealing fellows are all wrapped up in toasting warm wool, ready to play in the snow. They are both 27cm (10½″) tall, and can either be made from cast off woollen garments, or knitted up from yarn odds and ends. The basic shape is so simple that it lends itself to dress-up ideas such as scarves, hats, gloves and shoes.

Snug and Cozy

(Pattern see page 110)

These figures are both 27cm (10½″) high and made from pieces cut from knitted garments. First attach the head pieces, then sew the back to the front, incorporating the arms and turn out. If knitting the pieces up yourself, begin with separate legs, work for 4cm (1½″) in stocking stitch for the doll, reversed stocking stitch for the clown, and then join the two sets of stitches for the body. Change color for the head, and continue in reversed stocking stitch for both toys. Work the arms to match the body and attach on each side.

For the purple cap work a strip of knit 1, purl 1 rib,

11cm (4¼″) wide and 35cm (13¾″) long; sew together at centre back. The yellow cap is in knit 2, purl 2 rib (or use the wrist end of a pullover sleeve). Draw the last row of stitches up with a thread and place a pompon on top.

A strip of two rows of treble crochet (single crochet U.S.), 50cm (20″) long, joined at the ends, then gathered on the inner edge, makes the clown's frill. Make pompons for his front the same size as the one on the cap. The striped scarf is worked in knit 1, purl 1 rib and is 3cm (1⅛″) wide by 50cm (20″) long.

Petra and Paul

If you've already made a puppet theatre (see page 32) these colorful characters could make a good addition to your troupe of actors. As with some of the other puppets mentioned previously, Petra and Paul can also be stuffed and used as soft toys, or else act as gift wraps to conceal presents inside their bodies. However you choose to use them, they are sure to give much pleasure.

Petra and Paul

(Pattern page 111)

You don't have to have a puppet theatre to make these; children will play happily with just a single glove puppet. For the clothing you need 35g (1½oz), for head and hands 15g (½oz) of yarn. The hair is made up of oddments, according to the hair-style.

First knit the clothes and sew together at sides and shoulders. Then make a 2cm (½″) hem on the lower edges.

Hands: pick up the stiches on the ends of the sleeves onto 4 needles and knit for 3.5cm (1⅜″) in stocking stitch, then knit 2 together all round, knit 1 round, then knit 2 together all round. Draw up the remaining stitches.

Head: pick up the stitches around the neck of the cloth-ing on four needles. Work 5 rounds in knit 1, purl 1 rib. 6th round: knit together every other stitch. 7th and 8th rounds: knit. 9th round: knit together every 3rd stitch. Continue for 8cm (3⅛″), insert a 7cm (2¾″) polystyrene ball and draw up the stitches.

To give the finger a grip when playing with the puppet bore into the bottom of the ball with the end of a wooden spoon.

Hair: sew on bundles of yarn (see page 14). For the girl use 50cm (20″) lengths, for the boy 13cm (5″) lengths. Cut girl's hair into a fringe in front and braid the re-mainder. Glue on 10mm (⅜″) eyes, 15mm (⅝″) rosy cheeks. Embroider mouths in stem stitch, noses in satin stitch. Hem edges of head and neck scarves

Dobbin the pony and Larry the lamb are both fun to make. Dobbin has been created from some knitted parts, and some parts made from cut-up woollen garments. His warm blanket is quickly made up in crochet, and he has a neatly braided bridle of which he is very proud. His friend, Larry the lamb is knitted up very quickly in a simple garter stitch, and he's 28cm (11") long.

Dobbin the Pony

(Pattern page 111)

A woman's discarded pullover should provide enough material from which to cut the body, legs and two ear pieces. The muzzle and inner ears are cut from contrasting scraps. Mane, and tail about 35g (1½oz) of yarn; the bridle and blanket are made from gaily-colored oddments.

First put on the muzzle, then sew all around the body, leaving an opening where the mane will go. Attach the legs and the lined ears after stuffing. The mane consists of 23 bundles of yarn, each made from about 10 × 15cm (6") lengths (see page 14). The tail is a 17cm (6¾") tassel, knotted at the beginning. Nostrils and mouth are embroidered in stem stitch; the eyes are 25/20mm (1/¾") felt disks.

The bridle is a braid, 65cm (25½") long, made with 3 × 6 strands of yarn, the ends secured under the mane. The blanket, worked in double crochet (single crochet U.S.), is 13cm (5") wide and 25cm (10") long and finished with a woollen fringe.

The feet are made from a thicker woollen fabric, stuffed and sewn onto the legs.

The horse is a good project to do with a child; you sew the animal, while the child makes the bridle, the wool bundles for the mane, and perhaps the blanket (this could just as well be knitted, or even woven).

108

Larry the Lamb

(Pattern page 111)

The lamb is 28cm (11") long. The body is done in garter stitch, using 50g (2oz) of thick, white wool (bouclé is particularly good). Sew together the muzzle, legs and tail, all cut from scrap material, either woven or knitted. Stuff all the parts and join together. Make up the ears and sew on. Embroider the nose with two rows of stem stitch in a V shape. Eyes are 20/15mm (¾"/⅝") disks.

From these patterns you will see that making animals in profile is not very difficult. All that is needed is a simplified likeness in outline, and the accentuation of characteristic features – for example the lamb's curly fleece, the horse's mane and bridle. Many other creatures can be made to this simple design by looking for ideas and simple shapes in pictures and picture books.

Woolly toys

General Instructions

Specific instructions for individual figures are given only when the working is outside the scope of this general summary, or cannot be clearly seen from the photograph. A basic knowledge of simple knitting and crochet is taken for granted.

You can make any of the figures equally well by a technique other than that shown in the photograph, if it suits you better: knit if you don't crochet, or cut up old woollen garments and sew them together if you neither knit nor crochet. When making figures this last way, there's no need to worry about the stitches running – once the pieces are joined, either by machine or with small back stitches, they will be adequately secured. Old, much-washed woollen items are often rather felted, which is an advantage in making toys. If a garment isn't felted, you can soon make it so by washing in hot water.

Hand-knitted garments can be unravelled and re-worked, or used for pompons if there is not much sound wool left in them.

The color combinations given are only suggestions. Use whatever you have and whatever pleases you personally. All the animals for which patterns are given can also be made from fur or fur fabric remnants, either alone or combined with knitting.

Patterns

The patterns are on a scale of 1:10. To enlarge them, simply redraw; you will find it most convenient to work in metric sizes, making every millimetre shown in the book 10mm (1cm). The easiest way to do this is to use squared paper from an exercise book, or the kind sold for dressmaking. Where an animal has a curved or point-ed outline draw straight guidelines first, indicated by faint lines on the pattern. For gently rounded shapes draw the pattern with straight lines, and round the cor-ners off by sewing along the dotted lines indicated (the surplus disappears inside).

The actual-size patterns given for pompon and wound-wool figures can be copied onto tracing paper.

For a key to pattern pieces see page 111.

Making up

Cut or make each pattern piece in the number indicated on it (for example, beak 1, eyes 2). If you are cutting out the pieces from woollen garments, allow an extra 1cm (⅜″) on seam edges. Pieces which are to be stuck into another already have a 2cm (¾″) allowance. Felt pieces need no seam allowance.

Stitch counts

These are only given when the shape of the figure is formed by increasing and decreasing, and so cannot be shown clearly enough in the pattern. As you will be working with remnants, and the particular yarn is un-known, these cannot be exact. But remember that a slight variation from the dimensions given doesn't matter at all.

However, if you do want to reproduce the pattern exactly, simply knit up a test square in the chosen yarn and so arrive at the exact number of stitches.

Because of the wide variety of types and weights of yarn, both natural and man-made, the quantities given for making particular figures are very approximate and meant only a a guide.

Spread the finished pieces into shape on a soft backing and press lightly through a damp cloth. Place right sides together and sew, leaving openings for turning and fill-ing. If possible put these where they will later be hidden by hair, clothes or other added features. Felt parts are joined with small running or overcast stitches, close to the edges on the right side.

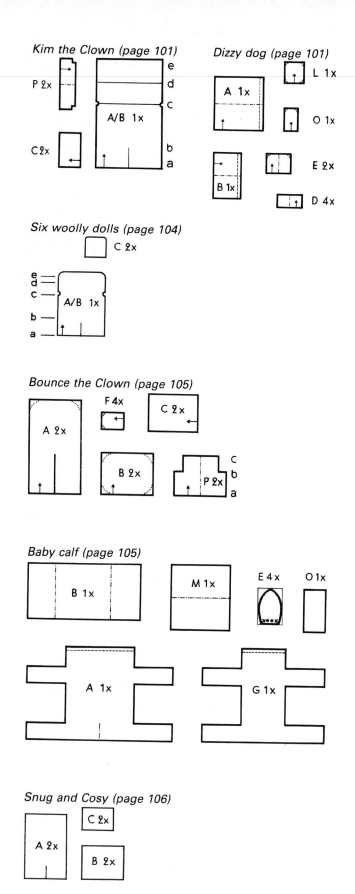

Kim the Clown (page 101)

P 2x

A/B 1x

e
d
c
b
a

C 2x

Dizzy dog (page 101)

L 1x

A 1x

O 1x

E 2x

B 1x

D 4x

Six woolly dolls (page 104)

C 2x

e
d
c
b
a

A/B 1x

Bounce the Clown (page 105)

A 2x

F 4x

C 2x

B 2x

P 2x

c
b
a

Baby calf (page 105)

B 1x

M 1x

E 4x

O 1x

A 1x

G 1x

Snug and Cosy (page 106)

A 2x

C 2x

B 2x

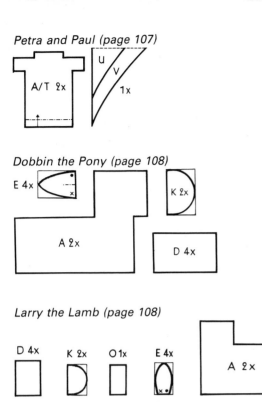

Petra and Paul (page 107)

A/T 2x

U
V
1x

Dobbin the Pony (page 108)

E 4x

K 2x

A 2x

D 4x

Larry the Lamb (page 108)

D 4x   K 2x   O 1x   E 4x

A 2x

Key to pattern pieces for Woolly Toys

A – Body
B – Head
C – Arm
D – Leg
E – Ear
F – Hand/foot
G – Belly
H – Body back
K – Front of head/face
L – Centre head panel
M – Muzzle
N – Trunk
O – Tail
P – Shoe
Q – Pullover
R – Trousers
S – Sleeve
T – Clothing
U – Neck scarf
V – Head scarf

Key to pattern markings

———————— = Outline or cutting line
———————— = Guide line
– – – – – – – = Break in fabric
–·–·–·–·– = Fold
- - - - - - - - = Gather
············· = Seam line for rounding off corners
•x = Fold with cross and dot meeting
←— = Knit or crochet in direction of arrow

Index